INCENTIVES
in the
NEW
INDUSTRIAL ORDER

WITH AN
INTRODUCTORY CHAPTER FROM
The Evolution of Modern Capitalism

By

J. A. HOBSON

First published in 1922

British Library Cataloguing-in-Publication Data
A catalogue record for this book is available
from the British Library

CONTENTS

ECONOMIC
POWERS OF THE TRUST

A CHAPTER FROM
The Evolution of Modern Capitalism
BY J. A. HOBSON

§ 1. It remains to investigate the actual economic power which a "monopoly" possesses over the several departments of an industrial society. Although the "trust" may be taken as the representative form of monopoly of capital, the economic powers it possesses are common in different degrees to all the other weaker or more temporary forms of combination, and to the private business which, by the possession of some patent, trade secret, or other economic advantage, is in control of a market. These powers of monopoly may be placed under four heads in relation to the classes upon whose interests they operate—(*a*) business firms engaged in an earlier or later process of production; (*b*) actual and potential competitors or business rivals; (*c*) employees of the Trust or other monopoly; (*d*) the consuming public.

(*a*) The power possessed by a monopoly placed in the transport stage, or in one of the manufacturing or merchant stages, to "squeeze" the earlier or less organised producers, has been illustrated by the treatment of farmers by the railways and by the Elevator Companies and the Slaughtering Companies of the United States. The Standard Oil Trust, as we saw, preferred, until quite recently, to leave the oil lands and the machinery for extracting crude oil in the hands of unattached individuals or companies, trusting to their position as the largest purchasers of crude oil to enable them to dictate prices. The fall in the price paid by the company for crude oil from 9.19 cents in 1870 to 2.30 in 1881, when the Trust was formed, and the maintenance of an almost uniform lower level from 1881 to 1890, testifies to the closeness of the grip in which the company held the oil producers; for although improvements in the machinery for sinking wells and for extracting oil took place during the period, these economies in production do not at all suffice to explain the fall. Indeed, the method of the company's transactions with the oil producers, as described by their own solicitor in his defence of the Trust, is convincing testimony of their control of the situation:—"When the producer of oil puts down a well, he notifies the pipe line company (a branch of the Trust), and immediately a pipe line is laid to connect with his well. The oil is taken from the tank at the well, whenever requested, into the large storage tanks of the company, and is held for the owner as long as he desires it. A certificate is given for it, which can be turned into cash at any time; and when sold it is delivered to the purchaser at any station on the delivery lines."[138] In similar fashion the Sugar Trust, before the competition of the Spreckles refineries arose, controlled the market for raw sugar. Nor was this power exercised alone over the producers of raw sugar. It extended to dictating the price at which the wholesale grocers who took from them the refined sugar should sell to their customers.[139] This power of a monopoly is not merely extended to the control of prices in the earlier and later processes of production and distribution of the commodity. One of the most potent forms it assumes in manufactures where machinery is much used is a control over the patentees and even the manufacturers of machinery. Where a strong Trust exists, the patentee of a new invention can only sell to the Trust and at the Trust's price. Charges are even made against the Standard Oil Trust and other powerful monopolies to the effect that they are in the habit of appropriating any new invention, whether patented or not, without paying for it, trusting to their influence to avoid the legal consequences of such conduct. There is indeed strong reason to believe that the irresponsible position in which some of these corporations are placed induces them to an unscrupulous use of their great wealth for such purposes.

§ 2. (*b*) Since the prime object of a Trust is to effect sales at profitable prices, and prices are directly determined by the quantitative relation between supply and demand, it is clearly advantageous for a Trust to obtain as full a power in the regulation of the quantity of supply as is possible. In order to effect this object the Trust will pursue a double policy. It will buy up such rival businesses as it deems can be worked advantageously for the purposes of the Trust. The price at which it will compel the owners of such businesses to sell will have no precise relation to the value of the business, but will depend upon the amount of trouble which such a business can cause by refusing to come into the Trust. If the outstanding firm is in a strong position the Trust can only compel it to sell, by a prolonged process of cutting prices, which involves considerable loss. For such a business a high price will be paid. By this means a strongly-established Trust or Syndicate will bring under its control the whole of the larger and better-equipped businesses which would otherwise by their competition weaken the Trust's control of the market. A smaller business, or an important rival who persistently stands out of the Trust, is assailed by the various weapons in the hands of the Trust, and is crushed by the brute force of its stronger rival. The most common method of crushing a smaller business is by driving down prices below the margin of profit, and by the use of the superior staying power which belongs to a larger capital starving out a competitor. This mode of exterminating warfare is used not merely against actually existing rivals, as where a railway company is known to bring down rates for traffic below cost price in order to take the traffic of a rival line, but is equally effective against the potential competition of outside capital. After two or three attempts to compete with Jay Gould's telegraph line from New York to Philadelphia had been frustrated by a lowering of rates to a merely nominal price, the notoriety of this terrible weapon sufficed to check further attempts at competition. In this way each strongly-formed Trust is able to fence off securely a certain field of investment, thus narrowing the scope of use for any outside capital. This employment of brute force is sometimes spoken of as "unfair" competition, and treated as something distinct from ordinary trade competition. But the difference drawn is a purely fallacious one. In thus breaking down a competitor the Trust simply makes use of those economies which we have found to attach to large-scale businesses as compared with small. Its action, however oppressive it may seem from the point of view of a weaker rival, is merely an application of those same forces which are always operating in the evolution of modern capital. In a competitive industrial society there is nothing to distinguish this conduct of a Trust in the use of its size and staying power from the conduct of any ordinary manufacturer or shopkeeper who tries to do a bigger and more paying business than his rivals. Each uses to the full, and without scruple, all the economic advantages of size, skill in production, knowledge of markets, attractive price-lists, and methods of advertisement which he possesses. It is quite true that so long as there is competition among a number of fairly equal businesses the consuming public may gain to some extent by this competition, whereas the normal result of the successful establishment of a Trust is simply to enable its owners to take higher profits by raising prices to the consumer. But this does not constitute a difference in the mode of competition, so that in this case it deserves to be called "fair," in the other "unfair."

It is even doubtful whether such bargains as that above described between the Standard Oil Company and the Railways, whereby a discriminative rate was maintained in favour of the Company, is "unfair," though it was underhand and illegal. In the ordinary sense of the term it was a "free" contract between the Railways and the Oil Company, and in spite of its discriminative character might have been publicly maintained had the law not interfered on a technical point. The same is even true of the flagrant act of discrimination described by Mr. Baker:—"A combination among manufacturers of railway car-springs, which wished to ruin an independent competitor, not only agreed with the American Steel Association that the independent company should be charged $10 per ton more for steel than the members of the combine, but raised a fund to be used as follows: when the independent company made a bid on a contract for springs, one of the members of the Trust was authorised to under-bid at a price which would incur a loss, which was to be paid out of the fund. In this way the competing company was to be driven out of business."[14C] These cases differ only in their complexity from the simpler modes of underselling a business rival. Mean, underhand, and perhaps illegal many of these tactics are, but after all they differ rather in degree than in kind from the tactics commonly practised by most businesses engaged in close commercial warfare. If they are "unfair," it is only in the sense that all coercion of the weak by the strong is "unfair," a verdict which doubtless condemns from any moral standpoint the whole of trade competition, so far as it is not confined to competing excellence of production.

The only exercise of power by a Trust or Monopoly in its dealings with competing capital which deserves to be placed in a separate category of infamy, is the use of money to debauch the legislature into the granting of protective tariffs, special charters or concessions, or other privileges which enable a monopoly company to get the better of their rivals, to secure contracts, to check outside competition, and to tax the consuming public for the benefit of the trust-maker's pocket. Under this head we may also reckon the tampering with the administration of justice which is attributed, apparently not without good reason, to certain of the Trusts, the use of the Trust's money to purchase immunity from legal interference, or, in the last resort, to buy a judgment in the Courts.

How far the more or less definite allegations upon this subject are capable of substantiation it is beyond our scope to inquire, but certain disclosures in connection with the Tweed Ring, the Standard Oil Company, the Anthracite Coal Trust, and other syndicates induce the belief that the more unscrupulous capitalists seek to influence the Courts of Justice as well as the Houses of Legislature in the pursuance of their business interests.

§ 3. (c) The more or less complete control of the capital engaged in an industry, and of the market, involves an enormous power over the labour engaged in that industry. So long as competition survives, the employee or group of employees are able to obtain wages and other terms of employment determined in some measure by the conflicting interests of different employers. But when there is only one employer, the Trust, the workman who seeks employment has no option but to accept the terms offered by the Trust. His only alternative is to abandon the use of the special skill of his trade and to enter the ever-swollen unskilled labour market. This applies with special force to factory employees who have acquired great skill by incessant practice in some narrow routine of machine-tending. The average employee in a highly-elaborated modern factory is on the whole less competent than any other worker to transfer his labour-power without loss to another kind of work.[141] Now, as we have seen, it is precisely in these manufactures that many of the strongest Trusts spring up. The Standard Oil Company or the Linseed Oil Trust are the owners of their employees almost to the same extent as they are owners of their mills and machinery, so subservient has modern labour become to the fixed capital under which it works. It has been claimed as one of the advantages of a Trust that the economies attending its working enable it to pay wages higher than the market rate. There can be no question as to the ability of the stronger Trusts to pay high wages. But there is no power to compel them to do so, and it would be pure hypocrisy to pretend that the interests of the labourers formed any part of the motive which led a body of keen business men to acquire a monopoly. One of the special economies which a large capital possesses over a small, and which a Trust possesses *par excellence*, is the power of making advantageous bargains with its employees.

It is possible that a firm like the Standard Oil Trust may to some limited extent practise a cheap philanthropy of profit-sharing in order to deceive the public into supposing that its huge profits enrich many instead of few. But there is no evidence that the employees of a Trust have gained in any way from the economies of industrial monopoly, nor, as we see, is there any *à priori* likelihood they should so gain.[142]

But the practical ownership of its employees involved in the position of a monopoly is by no means the full measure of the oppressive power exercised by the Trust over labour. Since the means by which Trust prices are maintained is the regulation of production, the interests of the Trust often require that a large part of the fixed capital of the companies entering the Trust shall stand idle. "When competition has become so fierce that there is frequently in the market a supply of goods so great that all cannot be sold at remunerative prices, it is necessary that the competing establishments, in order to continue business at all (of course, under perfectly free competition many will fail), check their production. Now an ordinary pool makes provision for each establishment to run in one of the two ways suggested. Manifestly a stronger organisation like the Trust, by selecting the best establishments, and running them continuously at their full capacity, while closing the others, or selling them, and making

11

other use of the capital thus set free, will make a great saving. The most striking example of this kind in the recent history of the Trusts is furnished by the Whisky Trust. More than eighty distilleries joined the Trust. Formerly, when organised as a pool, as has been said, each establishment ran at part capacity, one year at 40 per cent., one year at only 28 per cent. A year after the organisation of the Trust only twelve were running; but these were producing at about their full capacity, and the total output of alcohol was not at all lessened. The saving is to be reckoned by the labour and running capital which had formerly been employed in nearly sixty distilleries. It must be borne in mind that on the product of these twelve distilleries good profits were made on the capital represented in more than eighty plants. All the greater Trusts, such as the Standard Oil, the Cotton Oil, the Cotton Bagging, and the Sugar Trust, have followed this plan of closing entirely the weaker establishments and running only the stronger, thereby effecting a saving in capital and labour."[143]

Here we see a Trust exercising its economic power of regulating production. That power, as we shall see below, is not merely confined to closing the inferior mills in order that the same aggregate output may be obtained by a full working of the more efficient plant. Where over-production has occurred it is to the interest of the Trust to lessen production. With this end in view it will suddenly close half the mills, or works, or elevators in a district. The owners of these closed plants get their interest from the Trust just as if they were working. But the labour of these works suddenly, and without any compensation for disturbance, is "saved"—that is to say, the employees are deprived of the services of the only kind of plant and material to which their skilled efforts are applicable. It is probable that one result of the formation of each of these larger trusts has been to throw out of employment several thousands of workers, and to place them either in the ranks of the unemployed or in some other branch of industry where their previously acquired skill is of little service, and where their wages are correspondingly depressed.

From the account given above of the changes in organisation of production under the Trust it might appear that the effect upon labour was not to reduce the net employment, but to give full, regular employment to a smaller number instead of partial and irregular employment to many, and that thus labour, considered as a whole, might be the gainer. An industrial movement which substitutes the regular employment of a few for the irregular employment of many is so far a progressive movement. But it must be borne in mind first that there is usually a net reduction of employment, a substitution not of 50 workers at full-time for 100 at half-time, but of 30 only. For not only will there be a net saving of labour in relation to the same output, the result of using exclusively the best equipped and best situated factories, but since the Trust came into existence in order to restrict production and so raise prices, the aggregate output of the business will be either reduced or its rate of increase will be less than under open competition. The chief economy of the Trust will in fact arise from the net diminution of employment of labour. As the Trust grows stronger and absorbs a larger and larger proportion of the total supply for the market, the reduction of employment will as a rule continue. Of course, if the scale of prices which the Trust finds most profitable happens to be such as induce a large increase of consumption, and therefore to permit an expansion of the machinery of production, the aggregate of employment may be maintained or even increased. But, as we shall see below, there is nothing in the nature of a Trust to guarantee such a result. The normal result of placing the ordering of an industry in the hands of a monopoly company is to give them a power which it is their interest to exercise, to narrow the scope of industry, to change its *locale*, to abandon certain branches and take up others, to substitute machinery for hand labour, without any regard to the welfare of the employees who have been associated with the fixed capital formerly in use. When to this we add the reflection that the ability to choose its workmen out of an artificially made over-supply of labour, rid of the competition of other employers, gives the Trust a well-nigh absolute power to fix wages, hours of work, to pay in truck, and generally to dictate terms of employment and conditions of life, we understand the feeling of distrust and antagonism with which the working classes regard the growth of these great monopolies on both sides of the Atlantic.

The following is a short summary of the findings of a Committee of Congress with reference to the relations existing between the railroad and coal companies which control the anthracite coal-fields in Pennsylvania and the coal-miners:— "Congress has found (Document No. 4) that the coal companies in the anthracite regions keep thousands of surplus labourers in hand to underbid each other for employment and for submission to all exactions; hold them purposely ignorant when the mines are to be worked and when closed, so that they cannot seek employment elsewhere; bind them as tenants by compulsion in the companies' houses, so that the rent shall run against them whether wages run or not, and under leases by which they can be turned out with their wives and children on the mountain-side in mid-winter if they strike; compel them to fill cars of larger capacity than agreed upon; make them buy their powder and other working outfit of the companies at an enormous advance on the cost; compel them to buy coal of the company at the company's price, and in many cases to buy a fixed quantity more than they need; compel them to employ the doctor named by the company and to pay him whether sick or well; 'pluck' them at the company's store, so that when pay-day comes round the company owes the men nothing, there being authentic cases where 'sober, hard-working miners toiled for years, or even a lifetime, without having been able to draw a single dollar, or but few dollars in actual cash,' in 'debt until the day they died;' refuse to fix the wages in advance, but pay them upon some hocus-pocus sliding-scale, varying with the selling price in New York, which the railway slides to suit itself; and most extraordinary of all, refuse to let the miners know the prices on which their living slides, a 'fraud,'" says the report of Congress, "on its face" (pp. 71

and 72). The companies dock the miners' output arbitrarily for slate and other impurities, and so can take from their men 5 to 50 tons more in every 100 than they pay for (p. 76). In order to keep the miners disciplined and the coal market under supplied, the railroads restrict work, so that the miners often have to live for a month on what they can earn in six or eight days, and these restrictions are enforced upon their miners by holding cars from them to fill, as upon competitors by withholding cars to go to market. (Document No. 4, p. 77.)

Labour organisations are forbidden, and the men intentionally provoked to strike to affect the coal market. The labouring population of the local regions, finally, is kept "down" by special policemen, enrolled under special laws, and often in violation of law, by the railroads and coal and iron companies, practically when and in what number they choose, and practically without responsibility to any one but their employers, armed as the Corporation see fit with army revolvers or Winchester rifles, or both; made detectives by statute, and not required to wear their shields, provoking the public to riot (pp. 9 and 93-98), and then shooting them legally. "By the percentage of wages," says the report of Congress, "by false measurements, by rents, stores, and other methods the workman is virtually a chattel of the operator."[144]

§ 4. (*d*) Those who admit that a Trust is in its essence a monopoly, and that it is able, by virtue of its position, to sell commodities at high prices, sometimes affirm that it is not to the interest of a Trust to maintain high prices, and that in fact Trusts have generally lowered prices. We have here a question of fact and a question of theory. Of these the former presents the greater difficulty. It seems a simple matter to compare prices before and after the formation of the Trust, and to observe the tendencies to rise or fall. This comparison has been made in a good many cases, with the result that some Trusts seem to lower prices, others to raise them. The growth of the Standard Oil Company and the strengthening of its power was attended, as we saw, by a considerable fall of price. So also we are told respecting the Cotton Seed Oil Trust, formed in 1883, that "during these four years the price of cotton seed oil fell more than eight times as much as it did during the five years before the Trust was formed."[145] The rates of the most absolute monopoly, the Western Union Telegraph Company, are very little higher than those which prevail in England, where the Government works the telegraph system at a considerable loss each year. The Sugar Trust, on the other hand, directly it was formed, raised prices considerably. The same is true of several of the other most conspicuous combinations.

Now, it is argued, if it be admitted that prices have in fact fallen under the administration of some of the strongest Trusts, it cannot be maintained that Trusts have a tendency to raise prices. In reply, it is pointed out that in almost all highly-organised modern industries improved methods of production are rapidly lowering the expenses of production and prices, and that therefore the statement that Trusts tend to maintain high prices is quite consistent with the fact of an absolute fall, the question at issue being whether the fall of prices under the Trust was as great as it would have been under free competition. Moreover, a comparison of dates appears to indicate that the Trust's prices, as we saw in the Standard Oil Company, fluctuate with the degree of their monopoly, falling rapidly under the pressure of actual or threatened competition, rising when the danger is past. Finally, opponents of the Trust allude to certain Trusts which, in spite of the greater economies of production they possess, have raised prices.

Excepting by the inverse and questionable method of arguing that the high profits distributed by a Trust are themselves proof that prices have not fallen as they would have fallen under free competition, it is not possible to build a very convincing condemnation of the Trust from statistics of price. And even when profits are high it is open to the defenders of the Trust to maintain that they only represent the saving of the cost of competition, and that if competition were introduced the profits would be squandered in the struggle instead of passing into the consumer's pocket.

It is only from a deductive treatment of the subject that we are able to clearly convict the Trust of possessing a power over prices antagonistic to the interests of the consuming public.

A Trust, or other company, or a single individual who has a complete monopoly of a class of goods for which there is a demand, will strive to fix that price which shall give him the largest net profit on his capital. The question with him will be simply this, "How many articles shall I offer for sale?" If he offers only a small number the competition of more urgent wants among the consumers will enable him to sell the small number at a high price. Assuming, for the moment, that the production of these articles was subject to the law of constant returns—*i.e.*, that a few things were produced relatively as cheaply as many, this small sale would give the highest rate of profit on each sale, for the "marginal utility" of the supply would be high and would enable a high price to be obtained for the whole supply. But if he possesses large facilities of production it may pay him better to sell a larger number of articles at a lower price with a lower rate of profit on each sale, because the aggregate of a larger number of small profits may yield a larger net profit on his whole capital. How far it will pay him to go on increasing the supply and selling a larger number of articles at a lower price will entirely depend upon the effect each increment of supply exercises upon demand, and so upon prices and profits. Everything will hinge upon the "elasticity of demand" in the particular case. If the object of the monopoly satisfies a keen, widely-felt want, or stimulates a craving for increased consumption among those who take off the earlier supply, a large increase in supply may be attended by a comparatively small fall in prices. Sometimes a large increase of supply at a lowered price will, by reaching a new social stratum, or by forcing the substitution of this article for another in consumption, so enlarge the sale that though the margin of profit on each sale is small, the net profit on the whole capital is very large. In all such cases of great elasticity it may pay a monopolist to sell a large number of articles at a low price.

Where the article belongs to that class in which the law of increasing returns is strongly operative—*i.e.*, where great economies in expenses of production attend a larger scale of production, this increase of supply and fall of prices may continue with no assignable limit. On the other hand, where there is little elasticity of demand, where an increase of supply can be taken off only at a considerable fall of price, it will probably pay a monopolist to restrict production and sell a small number of articles at a high price. It is this motive which often induces the destruction of tons of fish and fruit in the London markets for fear of spoiling the market. These goods could be sold at a sufficiently low price, but it pays the companies owning them to destroy them, and to sell a smaller number which satisfies the wants of a limited class of people who "can afford to pay." Now, when free competition exists among sellers, as among buyers, this can never happen. It will always be to the interest of a competing producer or dealer to lower his price below that which would yield him the largest net profit on his capital were he a monopolist. If he is a monopolist he will only lower his prices provided the elasticity of demand in the commodity in question is so great that the increased consumption will be so considerable as to yield him a larger net profit. But if he is a competing dealer he does not look chiefly to the consumption of the community, but to the proportion of that consumption which he himself shall supply. The elasticity of demand, so far as his individual business is concerned, is not limited to the amount of the increased consumption of the community stimulated by a lowering of prices, but includes that portion of the custom of his rivals which he may be able to divert to himself. Hence it arises that under free competition it will be the tendency of the several competitors to drive down the prices to the point at which the most advantageously placed competitors make the minimum profit on their capital

§ 5. It is all important to an understanding of the subject to recognise that a monopoly price and a competitive price are determined by the operation of an entirely different set of economic forces. The loose opinion that it must be to the interest of a Trust or other monopoly to sell at the same price as would be fixed by competition is quite groundless.

Let us look more closely at the determinants of a monopoly price. Suppose we are dealing with a Trust owning a large amount of fixed capital, some of it more and some less favourably ordered for production, and having an absolute monopoly in the market for steel rails, cotton bagging, or other manufactured articles. First look at expenses of production. A very small output, though produced by the exclusive use of the very best machinery and labour, would not be produced very cheaply, because the economies attending large-scale production would be sacrificed. Each successive increment in output would involve a decreased expense per unit of production so long as the most favourably situated plant was employed. If the output grew so large that worse material or works fitted with inferior plant, or less favourably placed, were called into requisition, the economies of an increased scale of production would be encroached upon by this lowering of the margin of production. Taking the Trust's capital at a fixed amount, there would necessarily come an increment of output which it would not pay to produce even if sold at the price fetched by the previous increment. The ton of steel or of cotton bagging which would only yield a bare margin of profit, if sold at the price fetched by the last ton, limits the maximum output of the business. Under the pressure of free competition this marginal ton will be actually produced. But though, considered by itself, it yields a margin of profit, it will rarely if ever be produced as part of the actual output of a Trust. The actual output of a Trust, we shall find, will be determined at any point between the first unit of output and this marginal increment. The expenses of production will not increase in any close correspondence with the growth of the output, but will represent the fluctuating resultant of the several economies of production at the several points.

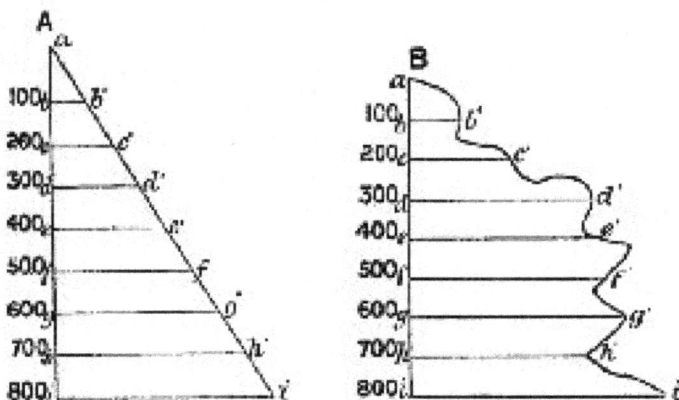

CURVE OF PROFIT IN TRUST.

In the figures A and B the perpendicular line *ai* represents a number of increments of production. The expense of producing a supply of 100 will be measured by the line *bb'*, that of producing 200 by *cc'*, and so on. But never in actual industry will the lines of growing expense be regular in their relation to the increase of production, as would be the case in the figure A; they will always be irregular, as in the figure B. The curve of expense *ai'* in the figure B will be determined by the resultant of the various forces which make for increasing and diminishing returns for each new increment of the requisites of production required to produce the new portion of output. When the increased scale of production makes some new application of machinery economically possible, or where recourse must be had to some decidedly inferior land for the raw material, a large sudden irregularity may show itself in the curve of expense.

When we turn from expenses of production to the aggregate

takings from the sale of the several quantities of supply, we shall find a similar irregularity of increase. Elasticity in demand, as tested by the stimulus given to consumption by a fall of price, differs not merely in different commodities, but at different points in a falling scale of prices. A number of equal decrements in price, according as they stimulate the satisfaction of weaker wants of earlier consumers, or strike into new classes of consumers, or supply new kinds of wants, will have widely different effects in increasing the aggregate takings.

We have then two widely fluctuating and highly irregular gradations of money terms, representing expenses of production and the aggregate price of the various quantities of supply, each determined by a wholly different class of considerations. But the interest of a Trust, as we see, lies in fixing supply at the highest net profits. Now the net profits of producing and selling any specified quantity of supply are ascertained by deducting the expenses of production from the aggregate takings. The relation between the growth of expenses of production and of aggregate takings will yield a different net amount of profit at each increment of supply. The diagram opposite will illustrate the nature of these relations.

AL is the line indicating at the several points, B, C, D, etc., proportional increments in supply. If the monopoly be a steel rail trust, B marks the millionth ton, C the two millionth ton of output, and so on. A'L' is a curve indicating, by its diminishing distance from AL, the diminishing expense of producing each unit of the increased output, so that the expense of producing the first ton, if only one is produced, is AA', that of the millionth ton, if one million are produced, BB', and so on. The expenses of producing one million tons will thus be represented by the figure ABB'A', those of two millions by the figure ACC'A'. Further, let the curve *al* represent, by its diminishing distance from AL, the diminishing price at which the several additions to supply can be sold, so that the first ton sells at Aa, the millionth at Bb, and so on, the aggregate price of the first million tons being ABba, that of the first two millions being ACca.

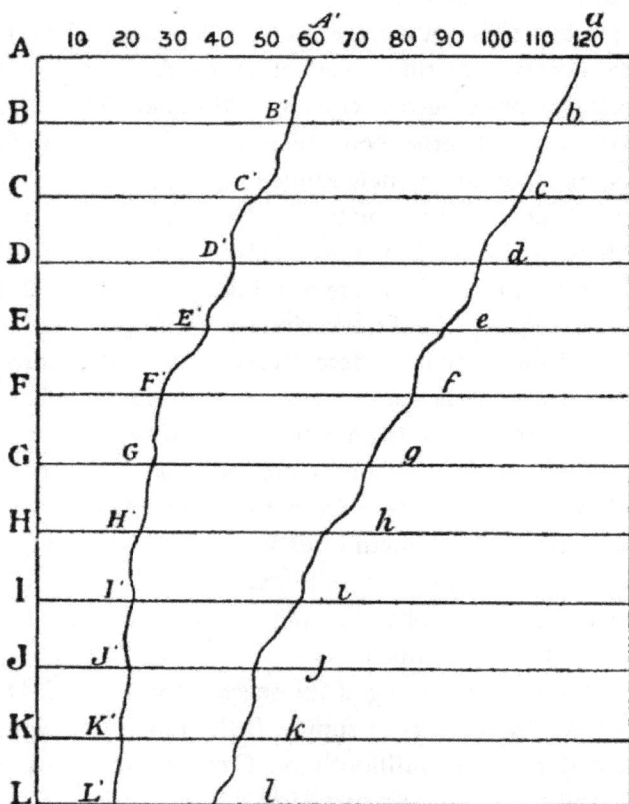

DIAGRAM OF TRUST PRICES.

Assuming that the Trust is planning a new business and determining the most profitable output, it will limit that output not necessarily at the point where the selling price gives the widest margin of profit upon the expenses of production, as might be the case at the point B in the diagram, but at the point F, where the margin of profit bears the largest proportion to the expenses of production, or in other words, where the area of absolute takings shows the largest surplus over the area of aggregate expenses. Thus it will here be to the interest of the Trust to produce and sell six millions (limiting production at F) with an aggregate expense AFF'A' and an aggregate takings AFfa, yielding an aggregate net profit A'F'fa. They will not produce five millions because the figure AEea bears a smaller proportion to AEE'A' than does AFfa' to AFF'A'. For a similar reason they will not produce seven millions.

Since the fluctuations in the curve of expenses and in that of selling price or "demand" are determined by an entirely different set of forces, it will be evident that there may be several points in AL where the proportions between the area of expenses and that of profits may be the same. So there may be several maxima at which Trust prices may be indifferently fixed. The figure upon F'f may have the same quantitative relation to the figure upon FF', as that upon H'h to that upon HH'. In such a case it will be a matter of indifference to the Trust whether it sells five million tons at a price 100s. per ton, or seven millions at 90s.

We have seen that the causes which determine expenses at the several points in A'L' have no relation to the causes which determine the selling price at the various points, except to furnish a minimum below which the price cannot fall. Above this limit expenses of production in no sense help to determine monopoly prices; the true determinants are entirely in the region of demand, and are measured by the marginal utility or satisfaction afforded to consumers by the several quantities which constitute supply at any given time.

Since expenses of production always enter into the determination of competition-prices, which are fixed by the interaction of expenses and money estimates of utility—*i.e.*, by supply and demand, it is evident that the curve of monopoly prices has no assignable relation whatever to the curve of competition prices, and that the most profitable output and prices of Trust-made goods are in no way identified with the most profitable output and prices in a competitive trade. In competition the curve of selling prices tends to follow closely the curve of expenses, and consequently the areas of profits and expenses tend to bear the same proportion to each other at different points of increment in the trade. For if at any point great increases in economy of production are achieved, while the large elasticity of demand maintains a price nearly the same as before, the wide margin of profit which might fix the actual price at that point for a monopolist only serves to stimulate such increased output on the part of trade competitors as will continue until the flexibility of demand weakens, and prices are lowered to such a point as will yield the normal margin or market rate of profit.

There is, therefore, nothing in common between competition prices and monopoly prices for different quantities of supply, nor anything to secure that the actual quantity of supply and the price shall be the same in the two cases.

§ 6. It is, however, conceivable that in a certain commodity where a genuine monopoly holds the market, the price should be as low as under free competition. This may be illustrated by the following curves of expense and price:—

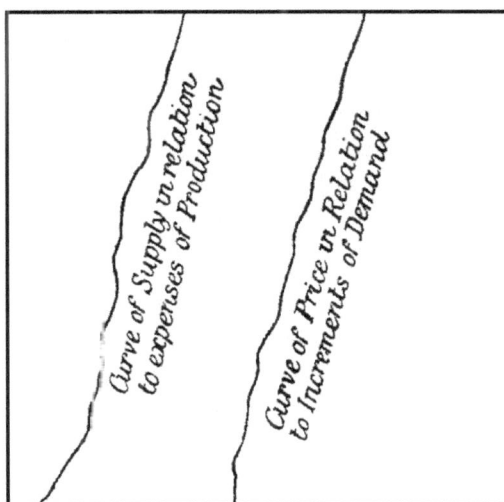

Curve of Supply in relation to expenses of Production

Curve of Price in Relation to Increments of Demand

where the economies of increased production continue to be very great, while the flexibility of demand is also high. In other words, it may pay the Trust better to make very large sales at a low price when the expenses of production are low, than to sell a smaller quantity at a higher price and with a higher expense of production. In this case the consumer may get a part of the advantage of large-scale production along with the saving of expense of competition. There is, however, no guarantee to society that low prices will be fixed. In the vast majority of cases it will probably pay the Trust better to limit production and sell at higher prices.

In the illustration above we have assumed that a monopoly was starting *de novo*. Where a Trust is formed, as is commonly the case, by an amalgamation of existing capitals largely embodied in plant and machinery of production, it will probably not pay to limit production to a very small output, even though the largest proportionate margin of profit might seem to stand there. For the interest upon the closed mills and other idle capital should be reckoned among the expenses of production for the purposes of determining the profitable price. Thus where large means of production are owned by a monopoly it will seldom pay to sell a very small supply at a very high price.

So far we have treated of absolute monopolies, eliminating all consideration of competition. We have found that the supply and the price of an article of absolute monopoly is determined by the relation between expenses of production and flexibility of demand. Although a new invention or a wide expansion of market may alter so considerably the expenses of production of the several quantities of supply as to materially affect monopoly-supply and prices, it is the latter influence, that of flexibility of demand, that directly in each specific case determines whether a Trust's prices shall be high or low. When we find the Standard Oil Trust maintaining a low level of prices, or the Western Union Telegraph Company charging low rates, we shall find the explanation in the character of the public demand for oil and telegraphic messages.

§ 7. A number of considerations relating to "demand" limit the economic power of monopolies to charge high prices.

A monopoly price, as we have seen, exactly measures the marginal utility of the supply, as indicated by the quantity of money which the purchaser of the last increment of supply is just willing to pay for it. When this marginal utility sinks fast with an increase of supply the monopoly price will be high for it, and it will pay the monopolist better to restrict the output and sell the limited supply at a high price, because a large reduction of price will not stimulate a proportionably large increase of consumption. So where the marginal utility sinks slowly, it will pay to increase the supply and lower the price, for each fall of price will stimulate a large increase of consumption.

Since the marginal utility of a number of increments of supply will not be the same in the case of any two commodities, it is evident that the determination of monopoly prices is a very delicate operation.

It is not possible to present even an approximately accurate classification of commodities in relation to the powers of a Trust or Monopoly. But the following considerations will assist us to understand why in some cases a Trust appears to raise prices, in others to keep them as they were, and in others even to lower them:—

(a) The urgency of the need which a commodity satisfies enables the monopolist to charge high prices. Where a community is dependent for life upon some single commodity, as the Chinese on rice, the monopolist is able to obtain a high price for the whole of a supply which does not exceed what is necessary to keep alive the whole population. Thus a monopolist of corn or rice in a famine can get an exorbitant price for a considerable supply. But after the supply is large enough to enable every one to satisfy the most urgent need for sustenance, the urgency of the need satisfied by any further supply falls rapidly, for there is no comparison between the demand of famine and the demand induced by the pleasures of eating.

A monopoly of a necessity of life is therefore more dangerous than any other monopoly, because it not merely places the lives of the people at the mercy of private traders, but because it will generally be the interest of such monopolists to limit supply to the satisfaction of the barest necessaries of life.

Next to a necessary in this respect will come what is termed a "conventional necessary," something which by custom has been firmly implanted as an integral portion of the standard of comfort. This differs, of course, in different classes of a community. Boots may now be regarded as a "conventional necessary" of almost all grades of English society, and a monopolist could probably raise the price of boots considerably without greatly diminishing the consumption. Half a century ago, however, when boots were not firmly established as part of the standard of comfort of the great mass of the working classes, the power of a monopolist to raise prices would have been far smaller.

As we descend in the urgency of wants supplied we find

that the comforts and luxuries form a part of the standard of life of a smaller and smaller number of persons, and satisfying intrinsically weaker needs, are more liable to be affected by a rise of price.

(b) Closely related to this consideration, and working in with it at every point, is the question of the possibility of substituting another commodity for the one monopolised. This everywhere tempers the urgency of the need attaching to a commodity. There are few, if any, even among the commodities on which we habitually rely for food, shelter, clothing, which we could not and would not dispense with if prices rose very high. The incessant competition which is going on between different commodities which claim to satisfy some particular class of need cannot be got rid of by the monopoly of one of them. This is probably the chief explanation of the low prices of the Standard Oil. As an illuminant, oil is competing with gas, candles, electricity, and unless the monopoly were extended laterally so as to include these and any other possible illuminants, the Trust's prices cannot be determined merely by the pressure of the need for artificial light. Though to a modern society artificial light is probably even more important than sugar, a Sugar Trust may have a stronger monopoly and be able to raise prices higher than an Oil Trust, because the substitutes for sugar, such as molasses and beetroot, are less effective competitors than gas, candles, and electricity with oil.

The power of railway monopolies largely depends upon the degree in which their services are indispensable, and no alternative mode of transport is open. Sometimes, however, they miscalculate the extent of their power. The high railway rates in England have recently led in several quarters to a substitution of road and canal traffic in the case of goods where rapidity of conveyance was not essential. So also in other cases sea-transport has been substituted.

The stronger monopoly of American railways consists

partly in the fact that distances are so great, and the sea-board or other water conveyance so remote, that over a large part of the Continent the monopoly is untempered by alternative possibilities of transport.

The reverse consideration, the possibility of substituting the article of monopoly for other articles of consumption, and so securing a wider market, has quite as important an influence on prices. The possibility of substituting oil for coal in cooking and certain other operations has probably a good deal to do with the low price of oil. A Trust will often keep prices low for a season in order to enable their article to undersell and drive out a rival article, a competition closely akin to the competition with a rival producer of the same article. When natural gas was discovered in the neighbourhood of Pittsburg, the price was lowered sufficiently to induce a large number of factories and private houses to give up coal and to burn gas. After expensive fittings had been put in, and the habit of using gas established, the Gas Company, without any warning, proceeded to raise the rates to the tune of 100 per cent. When we ascend to the higher luxuries, the competition between different commodities to satisfy the same generic taste, or even to divert taste or fashion from one class of consumption to another class, is highly complicated, and tempers considerably the control of a Trust over prices.

The power of a company which holds the patent for a particular kind of corkscrew is qualified very largely not only by competition of other corkscrews, but by screw-stoppers and various other devices for securing the contents of bottles. The ability to dispense with the object of a monopoly, though it does not prevent the monopolist from charging prices so much higher than competition prices as to extract all the "consumer's rent," of the marginal consumer, forms a practical limit to monopoly prices.

(c) Lastly, there is the influence of existing or potential competition of other producers upon monopoly prices. Where prices and profits are very high a Trust is liable to more effective competition on the part of any surviving independent firms, and likewise to the establishment of new competitors. This ability of outside capital to enter into competition will of course differ in different trades. Where the monopoly is protected by a tariff the possibility of new competition from outside is lessened. When the monopoly is connected with some natural advantage or the exclusive possession of some special convenience, as in mining or railways, direct competition of outsiders on equal terms is prohibited. Where the combination of large capital and capable administration is indispensable to the possibility of success in a rival producer, the power of a monopoly is stronger than where a small capital can produce upon fairly equal terms and compete. If the monopoly is linked with close personal qualities and with special opportunities of knowledge, as in banking, it is most difficult for outside capital to effectively compete.

§ 8. These considerations show that the power of a Trust or other monopoly over prices is determined by a number of intricate forces which react upon one another with varying degrees of pressure, according as the quantity of supply is increased or diminished. But a Trust is always able to charge prices in excess of competitive prices, and it is generally its interest to do so. It will commonly be to the interest of a Trust or other monopoly to maintain a lower scale of prices in those commodities which are luxuries or satisfy some less urgent and more capricious taste, and to maintain high prices where the article of monopoly is a common comfort or a prime necessary of life for which there is no easily available substitute.

FOOTNOTES:

[138]S.C.T. Dodd, *The Forum*, May 1892.

[139]"Trusts in the United States," *Economic Journal*, p. 86.

[140]Baker, *Monopolies and the People*, p. 85.

[141]Cf. Chapter ix.

[142]Mr. George Gunton, in writing upon "The Economic Aspect of Trusts" (*Political Science Quarterly*, Sept. 1888), claims a rise in wages as one of the advantages of Trusts, but Mr. Gunton throughout his argument assumes that a Trust is a large competing capital and not a monopoly. If a Trust were a competing capital its formation would be an economic and social advantage, tending, as he says, "to increase production, to lower prices, and to raise wages." But as a Trust is not a competing capital it does none of these things.

[143]J.W. Jenks, "Trusts in the United States," *Economic Journal*, vol. ii. p. 80.

[144]H.D. Lloyd, Essay on "Trusts," reprinted in *Boston Daily Traveller* (June 16, 1893).

[145]G. Gunton, *Political Science Quarterly*, Sept. 1888. This statement, however, appears in contradiction to the "Report of the Committee on Investigations relative to Trusts in the State of New York," p. 12.

PREFACE

A NEW Industrial Order is struggling into life, displacing piece by piece the old system of private capitalism over large areas of industry. That order was based upon unrestricted profit as the motive, competition as the method, the autocracy of the employer as the government. This motive, method, and government were qualified by considerations of usage, humanity and public opinion, the bargaining power of labour, and state regulations in the interest of workers, consumers, or the general public, but remained the dominant features of our economic system.

The recent rapid growth of combinations on the part of Capital and Labour, the strength of the Co-operative Movement, the financial needs and demands of the State, the frequency and severity of industrial conflicts, have led increasing numbers of people to realise the necessity for a radical reconstruction of industry. War experience has quickened this thought, as it has quickened the actual processes of change.

The New Order emerging in this country is neither State socialism, syndicalism, voluntary co-operation nor guild socialism, but a blend of these and other schemes, varying with the conditions of the several industries. But it embodies certain common objects: (1) the abolition of unrestricted profiteering; (2) the substitution of representative government for employers' autocracy; (3) measures for apportioning the product equitably and by pacific agreement among the parties interested in industry.

The workability of such reforms cannot, however, be taken for granted. The New Order is challenged by defenders of the old as impracticable, because capital will fail or fly abroad, invention, enterprise, and initiative will collapse, discipline will be slack in the workshop, and government interference will impair efficiency. Hence productivity will be low, and we shall be unable to maintain our population on a satisfactory level of subsistence, much less continue a career of industrial progress. These troubles, it is alleged, must follow the failure of economic incentives under the New Order.

My object in these chapters is to inquire into the validity of these and other objections, and in particular to consider how far private personal profit in present-day industry works economically, and how far it can be displaced by incentives with a wider, better, and more reliable appeal. Since this consideration of incentives involves the question of industrial control, I am led to certain necessary speculations upon the parts to be played in the government of industry by the workers, the employers, the capitalists, the consumers and the State, for the protection and advancement of their respective interests. The inquiry is informal and introductory, and presents no claim to be a scientific psychology of industry. I am indebted to Mr Delisle Burns and to my son for various serviceable criticisms upon the matter of the book when it was in manuscript.

J. A. HOBSON.

HAMPSTEAD,
   February, 1922.

INCENTIVES IN THE
NEW INDUSTRIAL ORDER

CHAPTER I

COLLAPSE OF THE OLD ORDER

UNTIL recent years in this and other industrially developed countries business life was conducted with considerable security and efficiency upon the following lines. An employer, or manager, with capital owned by him or entrusted to his charge, bought or hired business premises, bought the necessary machinery and tools, raw materials, fuel, and other appliances, and hired workers of various sorts of intellectual and manual capacity to produce, with the aid of these different appliances, goods or services which could be sold at prices which, after paying all these " costs of production," would yield a profit. The aim and end of a business were profit to be paid to the person or persons who supplied the capital. If the manager himself supplied his own capital, or hired it on stipulated terms, he did rot clearly distinguish the interest on that capital from the payment for his managerial work and enterprise. But where, as in a growing number of cases, the management was itself hired by the directors of a company of capitalists, the whole, or the great bulk, of the profit passed as dividends to the owners of the capital. The object of the employer was to keep down costs and to keep up profits.

In keeping down costs he met with several obstacles. The bargaining power of other businesses from which he bought his premises, plant and machinery, materials, credit, etc., might tax heavily his capital resources. The cost of his labour might be increased by Trade Union restrictions or " exactions," or by governmental regulations, or by shortages in the supply of efficient labour. In keeping up profits he might be hampered, not only by these high costs, but by falls of selling prices and shrinkages of markets due to cut-throat competition, tariffs and other political barriers, changes in consumption, or in methods of production in other trades which used the articles he had to sell.

His main skill and purpose lay in buying as cheaply as he could under these conditions, the articles he had to buy, including labour, and in selling the articles he had to sell at as high a price as he could get.

In order to keep costs down and profits up, he had to retain in his own hands all decisions regarding the technique and organisation of production, factory discipline, buying and selling, and the whole business of finance. Labour, alike of brain and hand, was simply a cost of production, to be bought by bargain in the labour market under such conditions of individual or collective agreement as prevailed. The government or control of a business was, in accordance with this scheme, definitely autocratic. It " belonged to " the person or persons who supplied the capital, it existed " in order to " produce profit for them. The services it rendered to the consuming public by turning out goods, and to the employers by furnishing employment and wages, were incidental and subordinate to the profit-making end. If more profits could be made, as sometimes happened, by restricting output, it was restricted; if by reducing employment or wages, they were reduced. Neither the workers regularly employed in the business, nor the public which had become dependent upon the purchase of its goods or services, had any legal or other recognised right or claim upon the business. The owners could shut it down or transfer it to another place, or alter its character in any way they chose, affecting vitally the interests of the workers or the local inhabitants or the consumers. But none of these had, or, according to the generally accepted view, ought to have, any voice in the matter.

We hasten to add, however, that the system did not work as badly as this bare account of it might indicate. The workers, the consumers, the public, were safeguarded in their interests to some degree by a certain amount of harmony, or consistency, between the profit-making motive and the interests of the other parties concerned. The theory of Adam Smith that " an invisible hand " guided the several factors of production (each seeking its own gain, whether in profits, wages, or prices) so as to co-operate with one another in turning out the largest quantity of wealth and to obtain for their share a satisfactory return, contained a considerable element of truth. So far as a fairly effective mobility of capital and labour existed, a fairly effective choice of their employment, a fairly free competition of buyers and of sellers in the several markets, the capitalist autocracy of business government, with a profit for its end, appeared to work with a fair amount of success and satisfaction. Taken at its best, with enlightened employers who had some grasp of the sound economy of high wages and other good conditions for labour, it seemed to be sufficiently successful to hold its own for an indefinite time to come. If high wages, short hours, low prices, and abundant output, could be got as by-products out of a system " run for profit," practical people would be quite content to go on with it. In other words, the claim for this competitive profiteering was that it provided a true operative harmony of interests and incentives for all the factors of production and consumption.

The universal and absolute validity of this claim, of course, was never pressed. It was evident that large numbers of workers had very little mobility, training, or choice of work, that much capital was limited in knowledge or opportunity of investment, that combination interfered with competition while landlordism and parasitic middlemen intervened between producer and consumer, piling up prices against the latter. But these defects in the operation of competitive industry were for the most part treated as " friction " to be overcome by the general spread of educational and other opportunities, or as belonging to the " accidents " that will occur in the best regulated societies. Only in the case of landlordism was there any clear recognition of a large factor of normal waste and obstruction in the shape of economic rent. All that was needed to secure the smooth effective working of our competitive system was free trade, free land, and free education.

Apart from the extreme views of a few socialists and other revolutionists, such was the accepted theory and policy of nearly the whole of the people in this country who concerned themselves with any general view of industry. Competitive profiteering, it was held, worked fairly well and with substantial justice and benefit to all concerned. During the latter half of the nineteenth century, at any rate, it has brought a large and pretty continuous increase of our national wealth and income in which all classes had in various measures participated. A prosperous and luxurious plutocracy was accompanied by a comfortable middleclass and a working-class which, in nearly all its grades and groups, had considerably raised its standard of living with a somewhat shorter worktime and more opportunities for education and recreation.

The complacency of this attitude was not seriously broken by the researches and revelations of the eighties into " Darkest England " and the slum life and sweating conditions of our low-grade workers in town and country. These evils, it seemed, might be remedied by philanthropic plasters, legislative reforms of an *ad hoc* character, and a strengthening of Trade Unionism. Not until the closing years of the century did the full size and stress of the industrial problem show themselves in a definite check upon the rising standard of the workers, and a failure of their economic and political machinery of self-help to remedy the trouble. It is important to understand that the new attitude of the workers in demanding fundamental changes in an industrial system did not originate in socialistic or other revolutionary propaganda, or indeed in any sort of intellectualism, though these teachings had some influence in the formulation of the new attitude. It was the concrete grievance of the stoppage and reversal of the wheels of working-class progress, the failure of wages to keep pace with the rise of prices, which began in 1896 and continued during the new century, that brought, first " unrest," then active insurrection among the organised workers.

The proved inability either of collective bargaining or of the new political labour party to secure substantial redress, and a growing realisation of the inadequacy of concessions in the shape of wages-boards, trade-boards, employment insurance, public health acts, and the like, went to precipitate the series of violent and costly strikes and lockouts which marked the years preceding the Great War. The experience of the war itself brought immense and swift changes, both in the structure of industry and in the psychology of the situation, as I shall presently explain.

. . . .

This brief rehearsal of pre-war history is

designed to shake the complacency of those who seem to think that the present large and even " revolutionary " demands for socialism, nationalisation, democratic control of industry, etc., are a mere by-product of the war, and that, when war passions have time to die down, and the industrial, commercial, and financial losses and dislocations have been repaired, our industrial system may be expected to return to its pre-war working.

As premises to any useful discussion of a new Industrial Order, we must recognise that the old order was already breaking down before the war, and that certain war-experiences, intended to be purely temporary expedients, have left permanent marks both on the fabric of industry and the mental dispositions of those engaged in working it.

1. Before the war, in many branches of industry, commerce, transport, and finance, effective free competition had given place to combinations close enough and strong enough to exercise a very real control over output and buying and selling prices. Great manufacturing businesses, banks and insurance companies, railroads and shipping lines, multiple shops and department stores were either swallowing up small businesses or (in order to escape " cut-throat " competition) were bringing them into agreements for an apportionment of markets and a fixation of selling prices upon a " fair basis " of remuneration. For the most part these agreements in this country were not " trusts " in the American sense, or " cartels " in the German, but somewhat looser structures, yielding more elasticity to the separate firms, often some

competition in quality of goods or services, but nevertheless amounting to a substantial interference with those competitive prices upon which advocates of the old industrial order of competition had relied for securing to the consuming public the fruits of the superior energy, initiative, and risk-taking, which they acclaim as the virtues of private capitalism. During the war the State controls and regulations, devised as war-expedients in most vital industries and services, accelerated and strengthened these processes of co-operation and combination among the hitherto competing firms. Though some of this enforced war-combination has disappeared, much of it has remained. The habit of working together by standard methods for a common purpose has disclosed so many economies of business administrations, that, taken in conjunction with the obvious interest of price-control in a period of grave financial and commercial insecurity, it has given a very important impetus to the pre-war tendency towards capitalist combinations. It is quite idle to suppose that the big combinations, especially in the metal and machinery trade, chemicals, and some branches of textiles and pottery, many trades supplementary to building, the railroad and shipping Conferences, are likely to return to free competition.

Free Trade and what is called the Law of Substitution may mitigate some of the dangers of these combinations to the consumer. But many sorts of goods and services are purely national or local in their markets. In other cases, as in steel rails, dynamite, cotton thread, and even some foodstuffs, where a world market exists, the art of Combination has become international. Moreover, the law of substitution itself sometimes is nullified by the tendency of a strong combination to spread laterally and take in the substitutional wares, e.g., as where a railroad secures control of the canals and road transport.

This growth of combination in many important industries removes or diminishes some of the incentives to efficiency claimed for the competitive system, and leaves the consumer without his former protection against excessive prices.

2. In many of the industries where capital has sought this protective shield of combination labour has followed the same policy, achieving a close solidarity for bargaining on wages, hours, and other conditions of employment. In 1890 about 20% of the adult male manual workers of Great Britain were members of trade unions, and in 1920 more than 60%. In mining, railways, engineering, most metal and textile trades, and in some public and semi-public services, such as postal service, electricity and road transport, combination of labour is virtually complete. Wages and other conditions are in most of these essential trades determined no longer by individual contract but by tests of collective economic strength between two combinations. Under such combinations the actual wage rates paid will not accord closely with the amount of strength or skill or training, risk, regularity of employment, or other special qualities of the kind of labour, but will depend a good deal upon the resistance of the combined capital. That

B

in its turn will largely depend upon the power to pass on high wages, or other increased costs of production, to the consumer in high prices. This power will be greatest in industries producing indispensable goods or services.

Now it is chiefly in these industries that combination both of capital and labour has displaced competition, thus leaving the consumer deprived of the natural protection which free competition used to afford.

3. There remains a wider aspect of the same change to be taken into account. Though it is in the great fundamental industries that combination has for the most part made the strongest growth both on the side of capital and of labour, the general spread of combination over the whole field of industry, commerce, transport and other services, with varying degrees of strength, brings out what may almost be regarded as a new principle of distribution. The remunerativeness of a trade, alike for its capital and its labour, comes more and more to depend upon the degree of the importance of its goods or services to the general public. This means that, instead of the strain of competition falling upon the several businesses and the several employees in a trade, it falls upon the several trades, which compete with one another by display of relative economic strength for the largest share of the aggregate income which they can get. Workers strongly organised in fundamental industries, such as mining, railways, electricity, where continuity of supply is essential to the life of the community, will under these circumstances

be in a position to get a higher remuneration than other workers of equal skill and energy in other industries. In some instances they may be able to divert into their class-wage what otherwise would have formed surplus profits for the capital employed in their trade. Indeed, the ability to get these higher wages will usually depend upon the existence of a combination of employers strong enough to fix prices and profits above the competitive level. For though in some trades, as for example the building trade, the strength of certain crafts has been the chief direct propeller to a rising cost of production to be passed on in higher prices to consumers, the most significant outcome of recent industrial experience has been the growing recognition of capital and labour in the well-organised trades that underneath the conflict over wages and profits there emerges a deep underlying unity of interest and a tendency towards adjustment of their respective claims by fixing prices at a level high enough to pay good wages and high profits. A trust or strong combine can afford to be, and often is, a " good employer " whose conditions for labour are up to or above the standard. In some trades organisation of labour is half-consciously directed to getting for the employees a share in the plunder obtained by charging " monopoly " or semi-monopoly prices to other trades, or the private consumer, for the goods or services which they supply. As organisation becomes more effective in the fundamental and pivotal trades, it must be expected that the mutual recognition on the part of the capitalists, managers, and workers of the waste from a conflict between these factors, will bring them into closer and more harmonious co-operation in seeking a common gain out of the public at large by sharing the gains from high prices. The capitalists, managers and workers in non-essential trades would under such circumstances be depressed in their remuneration, an increasing share of the general income passing in dividends, salaries, and wages, to those engaged in the powerful well-organised essential trades.

4. The pressure of labour for a higher standard of comfort, and in general for better conditions, has carried with it a demand, only half conscious in most cases, for some direct participation of the workers in the conduct of the business, or industry. This has moved towards the establishment of two new principles : first, the insistence that the workers have a vested interest in the industry that employs them; secondly, that in virtue of that vested interest, or property, they also have a right of representation in the actual government of the business and industry.

This is the most radical challenge to the established Industrial Order, the central principle of which is that the business is the exclusive and absolute " property," legal and practical, of the owners of the capital, and that the entire management and control, technical, commercial, and financial, is vested in the representatives of capital. This new claim to status on the part of labour has naturally followed from the habit of negotiation between organised labour and the employer or his

Association, a habit which has woven institutions such as Arbitration, Conciliation, and Sliding Scale Boards, in which organised labour is recognised as differing from other costs of production in that its sellers have a permanent interest in the business and a right to " a voice " in the conduct of the business so far as that limited interest is affected. This claim to " status " has also been attested in the case of Agriculture, Mining, the sweated industries and certain public services, by the action of the State in establishing Trade Boards, Wage Boards, and regulations securing minimum wages and provisions against unemployment.

Thus the purely *laissez faire* private contract principle, by which labour-power was bought and sold, like coal, raw materials, and other requisites of industry, in a free market, has disappeared from the higher and the lower trades alike, while the principle of labour's representation in some body competent to fix wages, hours, and other conditions, is widely, though not yet universally conceded. Recent war-experience has here too accelerated the movement. For though many of the wages, price and employment, controls have been removed, they have left a definitely heightened conviction that, as regards minimum wage and provision against unemployment, the rights and interests of labour must be safeguarded. The extension of the Trades Boards to a large number of fresh trades, emergency post-war provision of unemployed relief, together with a growing acceptance of the view that the responsibility for keeping its " reserve " of unemployed should be thrown wholly or mainly on the industry, involve on the part of the Government and the public a loose but real recognition of labour's demand for " status " and a voice in industrial government.

5. Governmental actions, however, have by no means been directed exclusively to assisting labour to a new industrial status. To an increasing extent it is recognised that the State, representing the consumer or the public safety, must take a hand in industry. The drastic interference in war-time, first with the financial powerhouse, then with an increasing number of vital industries, regulating supplies, enforcing co-operation, fixing costs, prices and wages, has left a strong conviction that in times of national emergency the State must and will intervene. Even before the war and since, the Government has intervened for the settlement of trade disputes, as guardian of the public interest.

The earlier disposition of employers and workers to resent such interference with their private quarrels and to claim that the State should merely " keep the ring " has been greatly modified by events, and though both capital and labour are still reluctant to admit compulsory state arbitration, the public sentiment against the claim of private groups of employers and employed to hold up the whole trade of the country and inconvenience a public which has no effective power of self-protection, has been growing sensibly.

.   .   .   .

These recent changes in the structure and operation of industry have had a profoundly educative effect upon the minds of the minority of men and women who seek not merely to follow but to form policy. But while they have broken the confidence formerly reposed in the efficiency and substantial justice of the old system, they have not established confidence in any system which should take its place.

State socialism, communism, guild socialism, and variants of these projects, have their enthusiastic disciples. But none has won the intellectual and moral allegiance of any large proportion of those who are opening their minds to the necessity and desirability of drastic reforms. Leaving out of consideration the doctrinaire adherents of individualism and private enterprise, I propose to address myself to the difficulties of a more practical character which among open-minded people block or obscure the acceptance of a new Industrial Order embodying the principle of public ownership or control of fundamental and essential industries with the principle of representative government in the several industries so owned and controlled.

For it is these two principles which are emerging in most of the new proposals, and most of the real difficulties raised against the new Industrial Order (to use the vague but convenient term) relate to the alleged impracticability of their application. But before we set ourselves to the consideration of the workability of the new Industrial Order, we must recognise that the old order of private competitive enterprise conducted by capitalists for profit has lost some of the securities and other advantages which it formerly possessed. Joint-stock companies, by limiting the liability of the great majority of capitalists, have weakened their incentive to exercise care in the investment of their capital and in the control of the business in which it is employed. Having limited stakes in a variety of different enterprises, most investors have neither the time, the knowledge, nor the opportunity, to exercise any personal skill, energy or initiative, in the conduct of these enterprises, which are left for the most part to a salaried management and a directorate whose sanction is required for a few major acts of policy. The body of shareholders normally exercise no real economic function after their initial act of investment has been performed, and the variations in the dividends they receive lie outside their effective control. The direct and real government of the business world has passed more and more into the hands of small groups of persons, financiers, entrepreneurs, managers, who wield the vast capital resources of great bodies of almost inert investors. Though these latter, as stockholders or bondholders, receive from industry in fixed or variable incomes a large proportion of the total gains, the productive utility of their industrial function is continually diminishing. It is an entrepreneur not a capitalist oligarchy that governs business under the modern system of private profit-making enterprise, and the profit which is the governing motive is not so much interest or dividends on capital as the personal gains of this active oligarchy. It is important to understand that capital has been treated more and more by the modern lord of industry on a par with labour, as a commodity to be hired at the lowest market price, in order that " profit " may be extracted from its exploitation. A misunderstanding often arises from the fact that the financier or entrepreneur is often himself a large owner and investor of capital. This, however, is not his primary function but an incident and a natural consequence of his profiteering career. The overwhelming majority of modern capitalists take no active, continuous, and useful part, in the directive or productive work of industry. In considering whether and with what degree of efficiency the necessary incentives to successful industry can be maintained in the new Industrial Order this will be seen to be a matter of critical importance.

CHAPTER II

MANY who will admit all that has been said to indicate the weakening or disappearance of some of the virtues and safeguards attributed to private business enterprise, may still remain of the conviction that the balance of advantages will turn in its favour when the workability of the new system is closely and impartially examined. On both sides, it may be urged, there are merits and defects. But the old system has been found to work with tolerable success, and will still be found workable when the false hopes regarding the successful operation of the new system have been dispelled. This I conceive to express the mind, not only of the wealthy conservative adherents to the old order, but of not a few who would gladly accept even the grave inconveniences which a rapid industrial transformation would involve, if they were persuaded that the new order would work better.

The comparative workability of the two systems is the issue. Let us set ourselves to this comparison. Industry is a complex co-operation of many kinds of human activities, each supported by conscious and voluntary human efforts. These efforts depend upon the existence of adequate incentives. If we compare the old system with the new, in respect of kinds and compositions of human activities required, they will not be found to differ very much. In other words, most of the same sort of work, skilled and unskilled, agreeable and disagreeable, physical and mental, will have to be done under either system. The change will be chiefly in terms of motive or incentive.

So much for generalities. Now for closer grip with facts and forces. The most convenient way of testing the workability of the New Order will be first to enumerate the various orders of activity involved in the working of the industrial system and then, having regard to such changes in this working as are involved in the new proposals, to consider separately whether each of the necessary incentives is likely to be forthcoming.

First comes a set of activities, mostly acts of thought and will, necessary to plan, maintain, improve, and direct, the material and human structure of a business. The plant and technical processes of every business embody innumerable inventions, ancient and modern, great and small. Much of this new knowledge, as it comes from the minds of thinkers and inventors, is not directly applicable to business. Either it is too theoretic or, if designed for application, is disabled for immediate use by expense, or by some practical defect. A certain type of business ability is devoted to looking out for such inventions and discoveries, selecting such as seem likely to contain some profitable economy, and after due experimentation applying them to business purposes. The value of this eye for profitable ideas and devices differs, of course, according to the stage in development a business has reached and the degree of its dependence upon new scientific progress. But everywhere in capitalist industry there is much scope for this kind of intelligence and judgment in the projectors and entrepreneurs. Indeed, the direct employment of chemists, engineers, business experts, artists, in order that new knowledge and higher qualities of taste may be available easily and without delay, is a distinctive recognition of the importance of the continuous application of new ideas to business ends.

What applies to the technical arts of production, applies also to business organisation, factory discipline, marketing, book-keeping, and finance. Everywhere new live thought must be available to make a business successful.

Critical actions of immense importance are often involved in the planning and establishment of a business. If the industry is young, or is in a period of transformation, these activities of thought, calculation and judgment, will determine success or failure. But even in industries which are well-set in structure and comparatively regular in habits, as certain of our staple textile, metals, building trades, to get a footing for a new business and to secure a market for its products involve powers of thought and will, which though confined in range and object, have high economic value.

The entrepreneurs who project new businesses or large transformations of old ones need, however, not only to put forth these activities of thought and judgment, but to obtain the use of capital in order to carry out their projects. They must secure the confidence of two other sets of people, first of some financial men, promoters, bankers or others, who are willing to back their judgment upon the success of the scheme, and secondly of the general investing public who must in the last resort supply the necessary money. Thus one realises how the establishment or enlargement of a business requires qualities of invention, initiative, risk-taking and enterprise, calculation and faith, to be given out by various co-operating groups of business men and investors.

When a business is in existence there will arise many opportunities for the exercise of initiative, calculation, judgment, temper. Large questions of policy in business arrangements or finance are sometimes put to the directors, and even in the last resort to the shareholders, when it is a company. But in the case of the manager matters of skilled calculation and of quick judgment are apt to be so numerous and various as to tax continuously certain active powers of intellect and character. Even in the most routine business changes and irregularities will frequently occur requiring quick and accurate decisions, if considerable losses are to be avoided or considerable gains effected. When, where, how, and what, to buy and to sell—upon an accumulation of such acts of judgment the success or failure of a business largely hinges.

Distinguishable from these rare or frequent acts of mind dealing with the initiation and the larger decisions of business life, there are the more regular activities of management and control, employed to obtain fullest and most productive use of the material and human equipment. Here, too, the human activity is directed to the maintenance of what we term the routine work, by checking errors or minor breeches of routine. This is, in a sense, the character of all human work. Exact work of repetition can be and nearly always is done by machinery, a few men being told off to correct any errors the machine may make and to feed it, where the process of feeding is not absolutely uniform.

But the skill and judgment of the manager is distinct in scale and character from those of the men under him. They are mostly concerned with the irregularities and wastes of machinery and materials. He is largely concerned in checking their irregularities or wastes, or conversely, in putting to the most productive use the employees. This work of organisation and of discipline probably must rank as the most distinctive work of the employer-manager. In large developed businesses much of it, of course, is delegated down a hierarchy of departmental officials and foremen. The main activity of most of these consists in looking after the men and checking errors, wastes, and slackness, on their part.

Labour has to give out continuously during the working day interrelated energies of muscle and brain in physical movements applied to processes of production. Sometimes the muscular factor plays a very small part, as in clerical and most distributive work. But a long day's work generally involves some measure of physical exhaustion and carries in its later hours a conscious cost. Although most industrial work is not, as we see, absolutely routine and repetitive, being applied to do what machinery cannot do,[1] the bulk of such work under modern division of labour is so narrow in the range of skill and judgment it requires as to overtax particular sets of nerves and muscles. The activities of labour then may be graded according to the measure of the scope for skill, judgment and self-determination which each kind of work affords. Mental work, i.e., that of a counting-house clerk, may be almost as distinctively mechanical as that of any machine-feeder. This is proved by the fact that much of it can be done, and is, by machines. But as a rule the pace at which it is done and other details of method are left to the discretion of the worker. It is the subjection to the machine, or to the arbitrary will of an overseer or other official, that adds so much to the human cost of most labour.

There is, however, a deeper element of natural recalcitrance against regular, continuous, specialised activity of any kind. Biologically man through his long primitive evolution was not " intended " for such work, but rather for short irregular and varied efforts. Everywhere he has been broken in imperfectly and with difficulty.

[1] It is often said that machines can do most of the work at present done by industrial workers, if the cost of human labour is high enough to make it worth while to invent and employ them. But this only throws back the problem one more stage to the labour employed in making these machines and looking after them.

THE NEW INDUSTRIAL ORDER

Long regular hours, minute subdivision of labour, mechanical routines are in this sense " inhuman." So far as they are required to enter into the activity of workers, problems of discipline continue to press. " Spirited workers " will no longer " put up with " the encroachments upon their humanity which habit and economic necessity formerly induced them to accept. This recalcitrance is one important factor in the new demand for " status." Certain it is that, making every allowance for further utilisation of machinery and non-human power in the dull, heavy, and disagreeable work, and for the abolition by law, or public opinion, of certain other forms of dangerous or degrading work, there must remain a great deal of work to be done which is not capable of being made pleasant or interesting in itself to those called upon to do it.

This citation of the classes of activity which enter into and comprise business on its productive side, does not, however, exhaust the statement of our problem. Among the functions of the employer or manager we have placed the marketing of the goods or services his business produces. But the maintenance, security, regularity, and sufficiency of this market chiefly depend upon factors outside this business or industry. The industry is concerned with the effective supply. But this successful operation requires an effective demand. The problems associated with this aspect of industry are sometimes sought to be evaded by pretending that when goods get produced, they must get exchanged and consumed without any other difficulty or friction than arises from miscalculation and ignorance as to what things are wanted and where, when, and in what quantities.

We shall, however, find reason to hold that a separate recognition must be given to the market as a factor in the industrial system, and that the motives which sustain and direct effective demand need special consideration, alike in the government of the several industries and in the motivation of industry as a whole. The wastes and defects of the present system we shall see are largely attributable to the failure of consumption, or effective demand, to adjust itself to the actual operations of production, and we must seek for explanations and remedies in the psychology of demand.

The Industrial System thus envisaged is a highly complex structure of human activities, proceeding from individuals and organised groups of persons, who contribute inventive power, enterprise, capital, organisation, and a variety of intellectual and physical activities to the shaping, moving, and marketing of commodities and the instruments of production, and a corresponding but much simpler set of intellectual and physical activities expressed in the effective demand for these commodities. The operation of all these producing and consuming activities in their due places and proportions depends upon the continuous and reliable play of incentives directed to evoke and maintain the several sorts of activity.

The problem of the practicability of our new Industrial Order, with its central features of public control and representative government, can only

C

properly be tackled in terms of these motives or incentives. If any incentive needed to evoke and sustain any of these essential activities is lacking, or is greatly reduced in strength, and no new incentive of equal efficiency can be substituted, the experiment is foredoomed to failure.

CHAPTER III

PSYCHOLOGICAL TESTS OF THE NEW INDUSTRIAL ORDER

IN order to prevent misunderstanding I will here repeat that, in discussing the psychological supports for what I call the New Industrial Order, I am not supposing any sudden general wholesale transformation of private enterprise into Socialism (State or other) or any scheme for the total abolition of private property in instruments of production. I am confronting the central facts of the new situation : (1) that free competition is no longer existent in some of our fundamental industries and cannot be restored ; (2) that in these industries capitalist combination, often accompanied by labour combination, has brought intolerable dangers to other industries and to the consuming public; (3) that public control of these monopolies or quasi-monopolies is recognised as necessary; (4) that reasonable distrust of central bureaucratic management demands that any public ownership or control be accompanied by representative self-government adjusted to the character of the several industries thus " nationalised."

People favourable to this line of movement will differ as to what industries should first be brought under the new regime, and how far and fast nationalisation should proceed. But without dogmatising on the subject I shall assume that coal mining, railways, and electric generation and supply, and probably the chief functions of banking and insurance, in other words the industrial and financial power-houses of our economic systems, must be taken out of the category of private profiteering enterprise and put under effective public control. There may be other services, connected, for instance, with the distribution of vital commodities, which cannot be safely left to private enterprise. But it is evident that no general theory of Socialism, dependent for its working on some large view of the feasibility of social service as an adequate economic motive, is likely to be adopted in this country.

This limitation of our proposals relieves me of any obligation to enter into barren controversy about the inherent value of the institution of private property, or the " proper " limits of the State. The present proposal is to " socialise " in this country a number of industries, each of which, on account of its monopolist or essential character, has already been socialised in some other countries, and to suggest lines of administration for these socialised services which shall overcome the defects which experience has associated with bureaucracy.

Now to readers of the last chapter it will be clear that the numerous activities which must contribute to the productivity of a business are not entirely separate in origin and nature, and that there is a good deal of interaction among them. The incentives to saving and investment of capital must be affected by conditions relating to profitable enterprise, rewards of invention, the efficiency of labour. The efficiency of labour, in its turn, is affected by the cheapness and fluidity of capital and the abundance of available technical ability making for the most economical production and the highest possible wage-rates. And so it is with the other activities and their incentives, their co-operation to a common object, the production of wealth, imposes a certain interaction and community of interest and purpose.

This by no means signifies that in any given business or trade, or even in the national industry as a whole, intelligent self-interest would discover a complete harmony, and that conflicts between capital and labour, or trade and trade, or producer and consumer, have no reasonable cause but are due to fractious ignorance. The labour engaged in coal mining or shipbuilding may well recognise the desirability of not encroaching upon profits so far as to let down the existing capital, or to prevent new capital from flowing in for investment. The capitalists engaged in these trades may see the advisability of paying wage-rates adequate to keep labour contented and to maintain a good standard of efficiency. But wherever the arts of production or the market prices are such as to afford some surplus gains for the trade, or any section of it, over and above those minimum incentives of efficiency, a conflict of interest arises and each party will endeavour to secure for itself as much as possible of this surplus.

In the national industry at any given time pieces

of this surplus, not forming the " costs " of, or incentives to, production, pass, in the various trades, to whatever factor of production is, either by natural position, by organisation, or by chance, in a stronger situation than the other factors. In our existing industrial system large quantities of " unearned " income thus pass as economic rent to owners of limited natural resources, as surplus interest or profit to the financiers, organisers, and investors who exploit some new invention, develop some lucrative market, or plan some strong control over a necessary of life or trade. It may well be admitted that there are business men who, as investors or entrepreneurs, will demand the opportunity of making large gains as a condition of applying their mind and resources to a business. But rents of ability, as well as of superior opportunity, are often taken by industrialists, merchants, and professional men, far exceeding the necessary incentives to evoke the use of their special ability.

I dwell upon this existence in our present system of a large amount of unearned and economically unnecessary income, because it marks and measures a failure of true harmony and economy of economic incentives in that system.

The nature of this failure of incentives will require a closer analysis. At present I adduce the bare fact as a testimony to the undeniable defect and waste of motives in our current industrial system, because these facts have an obvious bearing upon the consideration of the working of the new Industrial Order.

For it devolves upon the critics and opponents

of that Order not merely to show that some of the economic incentives are weak or otherwise defective, but that these defects are as grave as, or graver than, those from which existing industry suffers.

Bearing this in mind, and having regard to the interaction of economic activities, it may be profitable to call into special prominence a few of the broad objections most commonly adduced as fatal to the practicability of the New Order. I will state them briefly as follows :

1. The want of any safe and adequate provision for financing the socialised industries.
2. The failure of any industrial government or management in which labour is predominant or strong, or into which State interference enters, to apply adequate incentives to secure the best services of inventors, scientific experts, technical, administrative, commercial, and financial ability.
3. Defective discipline in mine, factory, field or workshop, and a related slackness and inefficiency of labour.
4. Bureaucratic incompetence, formalism, and corruption in any public ownership and control of industry, whether operated by central officials or by trade parliaments.
5. Inadequate protection of the Consumer against the domination of Producers.

There are, of course, many other objections brought by the adherents of the present system of free private enterprise against Socialism and industrial democracy. But some of them are inapplicable to the limited policy of Nationalisation we have here under consideration, while most others can easily be brought under the five types above cited.

. . . .

There are sound reasons for beginning our inquiry, by consideration of the incentives to saving, investment, and finance under the New Order. For the term capital rightly assumes a place of pre-eminence in the system which it is desired to displace. The badge of modern industrialism is the enlarged part played by capital in its various concrete forms of machinery and plant, power, materials, and money. The owners and furnishers of capital are the sole legal possessors and rulers of the greater part of modern industry, and the complex co-operation of economic factors is directed to the end of obtaining interest and profit for them.

The provision of the original capital of the undertaking, its maintenance by means of a replacement fund, a reserve from which to meet exceptional demands, fresh supplies of capital for the enlargement and improvement of the plant and output—these financial operations will be as essential in the case of nationally owned as of private enterprises. Will they be as effectively secured?

The finance of the act of nationalisation involves no difficulty, assuming that the private undertaking is taken over at a reasonable valuation. No new capital would be created. The State would simply assume the property of the shareholders of the mines, or railways, or other nationalised business, undertaking to pay them a fixed interest in government bonds instead of a variable dividend upon their shares. The valuation, however, upon which the private undertaking was nationalised, would presuppose that the business could and would be conducted as economically under the new as under the old administration. Considerable economies would often appear to emerge from closer unity of administration and the suppression of wasteful forms of competition. Against these, however, are set the probability of higher wage bills and the general slackness of officials not interested in keeping down expenditure or in stimulating personal energy of the employees. Upholders of the present system insist that the wastes will far outweigh the economies of nationalisation, and that the State would probably be landed with the obligation to meet a large annual deficit for the mines, railways, and other national undertakings. This deficit could only be met by taxation of incomes derived from other industries, casting on them a new burden which must grow with every fresh step in nationalisation, and which in the end must bring the whole industrial structure to bankruptcy. A single industry of national importance can be subsidised out of the public purse, i.e., out of other industries, but a large and advancing policy of nationalisation cannot thus be borne.

If there is a grave risk of the failure of nationalised services fully to pay their way and to maintain adequate reserves to meet bad times, it

follows *a fortiori* that it will be still more difficult
to find capital for the enlargement and improvement of these services. And yet that is what the
growth of population with growing demands and
progress of the arts of industry require.
Nationalised industry must not merely keep itself
but furnish a fund for new capital expenditure, or
the State must find the money from other sources.
The case of railways is to the point. If the State
took over the railways, the question must arise
within the next few years of an electrification of
the system. It would be impossible for the State
to discount the whole of this cost in the terms of
purchase of the existing plants. Nationalised
industries must show that they can pay their way
and set aside or borrow money which they can put
to such good use as will enable them to pay interest
upon the enlarged capital, or else the experiment
must break down.

Here is the acid test of the whole policy. Can
the State which has assumed the ownership of the
industry throw upon the industry as a self-
governing unity the obligation to provide normally
out of its own resources adequate pecuniary
incentives to all its employees, together with a
sufficient replacement and improvement fund,
without imposing an injurious burden of high
charges on the consumer for the goods or services
it provides? I insert here the qualifying term
" normally " because it is unreasonable to expect
a trade or other service to meet extra expenses,
damages or wastes, incurred as consequences of
public policies (such as war) determined by the

Government or nation. But a system of self-governing public services must be self-supplying in the sense of paying their way out of their own resources in ordinary times. No system of subsidies, either for meeting current deficits or for improvements, is a possible finance where nationalisation has passed into a wide policy.

This self-sufficient finance of a public industry, as envisaged in our scheme, thus relies upon an efficient economy of co-operation among the various grades of brain and hand workers represented in the industry, with due consideration to the interests of consumers as voiced by their representatives, or in the last resort by the arbitrament of the State as the final guardian of the public safety. For in considering the finance of such a public industry there emerges at once the possibility of a dangerous conflict of interest between producer and consumer within the representative body upon which both parties sit. The temptation of the producers to overpay themselves and to maintain their trade in a favourable state at the expense of the consumers will be very real. For though there will remain in the reduction of demand a check upon the extent to which they may raise prices, that check may be a quite insufficient safeguard for the consumers, especially where the goods or services sold are necessaries. It seems evident that in a governing body of the trade, the consumers' votes and interests may be overborne by those of the producers'. The State, therefore, as representing the public safety must be accredited with a final voice.

THE NEW INDUSTRIAL ORDER

The difficulties involved in this situation must be faced. The producers in a national industry, e.g., mines or rails, outvoting the consumers in the price of coals or rates of carriage, may say to the State " We cannot cut down our running expenses and we cannot meet them unless you let us raise our prices." The State must clearly be in a position to say " Your payments for such and such salaries or wages are unduly high, having regard to wages in other industries. Your demand is in reality a claim to have your employees subsidised by the employees of other trades. That course is unreasonable and opposed to public policy." It is clear that a self-government for a national industry must be devised that is compatible with the exercise of such a veto by the State.

But it is probable that the State will be called upon to exercise a further financial control in the shape of an authorisation of loans for new capital. For it is unreasonable to expect that a nationalised industry will be able to provide from its annual revenue for large new capital expenditure. As in the case of private companies, it must come to the general investing public for its money. But, if the ownership of the industry is vested in the Government, the new capital must be raised by the Government to be administered under the same system of industrial government as the original capital. In raising this new capital for, say, electrification of the railroads, or the exploitation of new mines, the Government would have to weigh two considerations. The first is the capacity of the railroad or mining industry to defray from its annual income the additional interest charges for the new loan, without raising the prices or rates of its commodities so as to press too heavily upon other trades and the general consumer. The other consideration is one which opens up a wider view of State finance. It consists in weighing the claims of a particular industry for a use of the borrowing powers of the State against the claims of other industries operative now or in the near future.

For though it be estimated that the industry in question is conducted so efficiently and economically as to be able to meet from its revenue the new interest charge, the borrower will be the Government, and the risk attending the investment must be assumed directly by the State, which, in the event of the failure of the industry to meet its new obligations, at any rate during the period of the new development, would be called upon to make good out of its general tax resources. Now at any given time the Government would only feel justified in incurring a certain amount of this financial risk. It might, therefore, be obliged to choose between the claims of several national industries seeking new capital, and to apportion between them the total sum which it felt able to raise.

This financial economy would, however, rest in no small measure upon the size of the total saving fund of the community available for such forms of investment.

Here we encounter a frontal attack upon the New Order by the defenders of the old. " You are still obliged to look to the savings of the private investors for the flow of new capital continuously required to enlarge and improve the fabric of industry, public and private. But the policy you are pursuing will inevitably check saving, divert the saving that does take place into foreign investments, produce a scarcity of capital within this country and a high rate of interest, thus crippling enterprise alike in public and in private industry." The checks upon saving, it is argued, are two.

In the first place, the policy of nationalisation of industries, price control and progressive taxation of profits, to which it is proposed to commit us, will, by destroying the prospect of high dividends and other prizes for successful investment, weaken the general incentives to saving in the community. Secondly, so far as this policy operates towards an equalisation of incomes, by preventing or cutting down large incomes, or raising the lower incomes by the action of wage-boards or public subventions, or both, it reduces the proportion of the general income that is saved. Economists have generally held that the unequal distribution of a given national income favours saving.[1] The rich can and do save a larger proportion of their incomes than the poor. For the " thrift " by which the income of the rich, after their normal standard of luxurious consumption is provided, automatically accumulates for investment, is an easy virtue compared with the thrift of

[1] *Cf.* Keynes, " The Economic Consequences of the Peace," p. 19; Stamp, " Principles of Taxation," p. 164.

the poor which means a deprivation of some necessary or some keenly desired comfort.

Here is opened an issue of transcendent importance in its bearing upon the economic validity of the whole new social economic policy. The defenders of the existing order assert that any and all proposals making for the equalisation of wealth and income by nationalisation, high taxation and rising wages, stop the creation of new capital and thus paralyse industrial progress. This line of argument has been persistently adopted by the assailants of E. P. D. who claim that this tax removes from industry a large part of the fund from which new capital would have been provided. Only out of large surplus incomes can large improvements be made or large new enterprises be undertaken, and the opportunity of making large " scoops " is necessary to evoke the spirit of business adventure and initiative.

Let us clearly realise the nature of this challenge put out by the defenders of our present social-economic order. They do not, indeed cannot, deny that large parts of the incomes of the rich are either payments for no personal services rendered, as in the case of economic rent of land, or payments in excess of what is necessary to evoke the use of the capital or business or professional ability applied to production, or are of the nature of business windfalls, inheritances, or other adventitious gains. But these unearned gains, they contend, are economically justified as being the sources and the stimuli of the growth of capital upon which economic progress depends. Progress thus appears to be based upon economic inequalities and injustice. This defence of unearned surpluses as the incentive and the source of economic progress takes the revolutionary bull by the horns.

Now can it be true that a new social order, with its monopolies nationalised, its inheritances and its high incomes heavily taxed, its rates of remuneration moving towards equality, would be rendered unworkable by this stoppage of saving and of increased productivity? All radical economists have hitherto assumed that any unearned surplus must be wasteful in its effects upon production, though they have differed widely in the meaning they assigned to this surplus. Some have confined it to annual land values, others have included the proceeds of State monopolies or other privileges, or of natural or artificial scarcities, or of inherited wealth and other windfalls.

The orthodox economists of this and most countries have agreed that the general income contained some such elements of waste which could be taken by the State in taxation without disturbing any current incentives to production. More radical economists (outside the socialistic circle) have pointed out that the existence of such surplus income diminishes in two ways the productivity of the nation. First, by enabling and inducing its recipients to live in idleness, or in useless or wasteful activities, it withdraws from production the personal labour represented by this leisure class. Secondly, this surplus income, diverted into other channels, as for instance into higher wages, might raise the physical standard of efficiency or evoke a larger output of voluntary effort in a class of workers. Thus it would be converted from waste into productivity.

This reasoning, however, does not meet directly the charge that capital will shrink under the new regime. Equalise incomes and tax surpluses, you reduce the investment fund! Does this necessarily follow? I set against this statement the proposition that a wasteful distribution of income involves a wasteful utilisation of capital. The easy automatic accumulation of unspent incomes of the rich in saving and investment, so far from being the instrument and source of future increased productivity, is quite visibly and intelligibly the cause of a needlessly low productivity. In other words, it embodies an attempt to save and apply to capital a larger proportion of the general income than can actually function as capital for the purpose of producing the consumable goods which under these circumstances can get effectively demanded and consumed. What we witness in normal times is a slowing down and a hold up of general production every few years, known as trade depression, during which large masses of the capital that has been accumulated stands idle, involving a corresponding reduction in employment and production in the part of all the other factors of production.

My contention is that this is due to a maldistribution of income which disturbs the just economic balance between saving and spending, and by enlarging the former while contracting the latter, produces and operates the means of turning

D

out consumable goods at a faster pace than they can or do get consumed. In other words, a chronic under-consumption, seen pre-eminently in the manufacturing industries, produces those periodic gluts and stoppages which are the source of so much waste, poverty, and misery all through the industrial world. The facile reply that general over-production is impossible, because everything produced belongs to somebody who, the wants of man being illimitable, will either desire to consume it or consume something else in exchange for it, is demonstrably fallacious. General over-production, congestion and stoppage or under-production, are familiar phenomena in modern trade. They are *seen* to be due to the inability of large populations, with the desire to consume the goods that are produced, to buy and consume them because of the lack of incomes or purchasing power. The present unemployment of capital and labour in most countries is a striking manifestation of this failure of effective demand, not invalidated in its economic significance by the political events with which it is associated.

Somebody undoubtedly possesses the pecuniary power to consume whatever is or can be produced.[1] But he may be unwilling to consume enough of it. Instead of consuming the quantity of commodities he could consume, he may want to pay persons to put up more mills and machines and fill them with more raw materials, i.e., he may wish to save instead of spending. Now if enough men with large incomes follow this line, the rate at which

[1] *Pace* Major Douglas, " Economic Democracy."

this new fixed and circulating capital may be provided and operated will exceed the rate at which consumption can be effected. True there are checks upon this wasteful procedure. Excessive and wasteful saving reduces the rate of interest. But this check is slow in operation. For falling interest does not proportionately reduce saving. There are several different inducements to save. Some of them, for instance the desire to lay up enough to live on in old age, may be strengthened by a fall of interest which means that more must be saved in order to attain the end. Much automatic saving of excessive incomes will go on almost irrespective of shifts in rate of interest.

But granting that the rate of interest does tend slowly to correct a tendency to over-saving, this correction takes some time and is not effective until much waste of productive power has been incurred.

There is another check, viz., falling prices. When production begins to outrun consumption, the fall of prices should stimulate consumption and restore the equilibrium of supply and demand. Here again we have a method of adjustment, real but slow, imperfect, and inadequate. If, whenever prices of commodities began to fall from the beginnings of over-production, consumers began *proportionately* to increase their purchases, they would nip the trade depression in the bud. But this is not the way a fall in prices works. It does stimulate some increase of consumption, but not enough. For the standard of consumption of most classes is exceedingly irresponsive to prices charged. Consumption is more conservative than Production. This is a fact of primary significance in economic psychology. When, therefore, retail prices begin to fall by pressure from above, consumers save a little more, though the economic situation demands that they should save a little less. Not until the fall of prices has gone far enough to cause widespread unemployment, i.e., to reduce the general pace of current production, does the painful adjustment between production and consumption operate, not by stimulating consumption but by depressing production for a time even below the rate of reduced consumption. Thus both economic checks, the fall of interest and the fall of prices, work too slowly and feebly.

I cite these facts, not to sustain a theory, but as a description of what actually occurs in periods of cyclical depression. There may be other contributory or incidental causes, but they visibly operate in the way I here describe. The speculative element I add is the interpretation of depression as consisting primarily in an attempt at oversaving attributable to a tendency of surplus-income to accumulate in saving and investment at too fast a pace.

In a more equal and equitable distribution of income the proportion of saving to spending would not be so high. But this by no means implies that an adequate supply of new capital would not be provided. For though the proportion of saving to spending would certainly be reduced by any policy making towards equalisation of incomes, either through higher wages, or taxation of high incomes, it by no means follows that a reduction in the absolute quantity of savings must or would take place. If this policy made for fuller employment of the factors of production, and so for an enlargement of real income, a smaller *proportion* of saving might yield as large or a larger *amount* of new capital. And this, I contend, is a legitimate deduction from industrial experience. If the rate of production were constantly maintained at or near the maximum which full employment of capital and labour affords, the normal output and income would be much larger than is actually the case.

The quantity of " slack " or " waste " in the running of the present capitalist system is far greater than is commonly supposed. The most striking economic lesson of recent years has been the disclosure of the possibilities of output and real income under the hasty improvisation of the war-emergency. It was proved that when some four millions of the younger able-bodied men had been taken out of the productive system for military service, and several million more men and women had been removed from ordinary occupations, to be put upon the making of munitions and other war supplies, the capital and labour left outside these war demands sufficed to yield wealth enough to support the civilian population on a level, which for the wage-earning class as a whole was substantially higher than before the war. Though the well-to-do classes, no doubt, reduced their standard of consumption, the working classes, or at least four-fifths of the population, lived in a definitely higher standard of material comfort than ever before. How was this possible? The fact that we were borrowing from America in the shape of large additional supplies of foods and other goods affords no explanation. For at the same time we were lending even larger sums to our Allies and Dominions, which loans they took in British goods or in foreign goods for which we paid by our products. There was some considerable letting down of plant and stocks in some departments of transport and industry. To that extent we were living on our capital. But no large contribution to our stimulated consumption came from this source.

The truth is that we were turning out wealth from our productive system at a greatly accelerated pace, because for the first time in our history all the available plant and labour was being operated at top speed. This full employment and high pace production were directly attributable to the pressure put on to the industrial machines at the consumptive end. The Government was creating a new enormous demand for commodities, and also, as a consequence of the shortage of labour due to enlistment, was enabling the workers to increase considerably their demand for consumption goods. From these sources there came an unprecedented strain upon the productive system, causing its plant and labour (swelled in volume by absorption of " the unemployed," the addition of large numbers of women, old men, and children, speeding-up and over-time) to turn out a product at least 50% larger than the same industrial system yielded on the average in pre-war times. And this result was attained in spite of shortages of some raw materials, much waste from official maladministration and other errors inevitable in this hasty improvisation of war-controls.

I am not arguing that this high war-production was desirable or capable of indefinite duration. What it testifies is this: (1) that a very large increase of output (real income) was attainable by a fuller use of the existing human and material factors of production; (2) that the direct efficient cause of this increased output was the enlarged demand for commodities due to a redistribution of income and purchasing power.

The Government took a large share of the income of the well-to-do and spent it, the workers took a larger share of the general income that was left and spent it. Even this high spending was not inconsistent with a considerable amount of saving applied to improved war-plant and other capital purposes, though no doubt not only the proportion of saving to spending fell but the absolute amount also.

But the lesson I deduce is this. If it were possible, by a somewhat similar peace-policy of high wages and large public expenditure on productive instead of destructive services, to maintain the volume of effective demand for commodities, not, indeed, at the war-level, but at a somewhat lower level, so as to relieve the excessive strain of war-production, why should not the capital and labour of the country be kept in full regular employment all the time, escaping the huge wastes of prolonged depressions and the minor wastes of ordinary times? If the productive system were kept working at say 80% of the war-pressure, the output of wealth (real income) would still be so much larger than in ordinary times that an increased quantity of saving would be consistent with an increased proportion of spending. In a word, out of a much larger national dividend, due directly to the incentive of increased demand for commodities, a larger quantity of new capital could be provided. The constant tendency of the machinery of industry to slow down, by reason of failure to find profitable markets for its full output, would no longer operate.

There should be no danger of a refusal on the part of the community to save as much as is required to enlarge and improve the capital structure. For the improved distribution of income which I am presupposing, though it would diminish greatly that investment fund which automatically accumulates from the surplus incomes of the rich, would exercise certain compensating influences ,which would evoke the economically desirable quantity of saving. It would have an important psychological effect upon the attitude of the workers towards the future. The insufficiency and the insecurity of livelihood from which most of them suffer are deterrents of saving. Sudden rises of " earnings " are " windfalls," to be spent as fast as earned. The habit of saving cannot be implanted under such conditions. Enough could not be regularly put aside to furnish any adequate provision for any great emergency, or for prolonged old age. Therefore, the savings of the workers are mainly devoted to short and cheap emergencies, such as burial, and brief spells of sickness or unemployment.

If the new social order could put workers in full security of a decent maintenance, with power to make adequate provision for retirement and for other lasting improvements of conditions, the saving habit, so common among fairly secure middle-class people, would take root in large sections of the workers. Part of the socially necessary saving done in this New Order would not take shape in ordinary processes of private investment at interest, but would be conducted by reserves or improvement funds accumulated by publicly owned industries in order to make provision for expansion. But most of the required new capital would still be got out of individual savings, at the rate of interest which sufficed to divert the required amount of income from spending into saving.

It might seem at first sight that this rate of interest must be much higher than before, because the surplus wealth which formerly supplied so much of it by easy accumulation is no longer available. In other words, it might seem to be a more difficult and more costly process to get the new capital under more equalised conditions of income. Reflection, however, will show that this by no means follows. The present working of the system remunerates all the new capital at a rate determined on the supply side, not by the easy accumulation of the rich, but by the cost of evoking the most difficult saving needed to meet the current needs of the system. Before the war it was necessary to induce the recipients of income to save about one-sixth of the annual national income to furnish the new capital required. Perhaps two-thirds of this fund could have been got at an almost nominal rate of interest. But the other third had to be extracted at some real sacrifice of present satisfaction on the part of those who supplied it. And since there could only be one market price for the whole supply, the easy saving was remunerated at a price determined by the difficult saving.

Now, under the new Industrial System, though the average sacrifice involved in saving a given proportion of the total income would be higher than under the old system, the sacrifice in doing the most difficult saving might be less, and when we bear in mind that a smaller *proportion* of this larger total income need be saved, we see that the price for saving, i.e., the rate of interest might be considerably lower than before. For not only may the subjective cost or sacrifice of the most costly saving be reduced, but, looking to the other side of the equation, the use of the new capital, we shall find large positive economies there. For if, as we contend, most of the wasteful competition and insecurity and slack utilisation of industrial capital are eliminated, an altogether higher level of efficiency in the utilisation of capital will be attained. Each unit of saving and of capital will have a higher productivity.

Again, though the supply of capital will be as necessary to public as to private industries, the substitution of social service for profit-making as the directive influence alters the incentives to the supply. In a public industry capital is hired on the same terms as labour at a standard price: its representatives no longer dominate the business policy. Capital is supplied in debentures not in shares, and is guaranteed a fixed rate of interest. The withdrawal of large areas of investment from speculative joint-stock enterprise into public securities will go far to rationalise and moralise the industrial system. For the speculative investment is not only a wasteful but a demoralising aspect of modern business, encouraging a gambling spirit among investors and dishonesty among financiers. Open-eyed risk-taking in new enterprises will remain a legitimate field of enterprise, but an ampler field will be presented to the more conservative savings which seek security and a steady return.

This consideration of the more conservative and rational nature of saving under a policy of more equitable distribution disposes, I think, of the objection that, if restrictions are put upon remunerative investments at home, too much of our new savings will flow abroad, seeking there the gainful opportunities denied here. There will doubtless continue to be many persons who like risk-taking and prefer to back their judgment or luck. If the field for such investments is restricted at home, the savings of such persons will gravitate to foreign countries. It may be recognised that this spirit of adventure in investors is within limits a genuinely progressive force, and it finds its legitimate expression more largely in new countries and new industries than in old ones. These fields of adventure will remain open to such speculative natures. At the same time the general tendency of a more equal distribution of wealth will be towards a more conservative view of investment and finance. For, as a larger proportion of the saving involves some real and calculated thrift, it will tend to play more largely for safety. The easily got and automatically accumulating savings of the rich will naturally furnish the larger gambling fund. Reduce that fund, saving will become a more rational process, making predominantly for safety of investment.

This differentiation between speculative and safe investment will itself favour thrift. The predominance of the speculative factor, by leading men to regard investment as a gamble, has deterred more saving than it has evoked. The saving habit is better nourished by a safe regular return than by a system of prizes and losses. The socially desirable balance between spending and saving in the general income will thus be better preserved by a reduction in the speculative area of industry.

Under such conditions the fears lest thrift, saving and investment, should fail to make provisions for industrial progress on its capital side, should be groundless.

A more equitable distribution of income would bring into play a better and more reliable set of incentives to saving under conditions which would provide out of an enlarged aggregate income a larger quantity of savings than before, though a smaller proportion of that enlarged income. In other words, the cancelment of large surpluses of income would stop the costly and ultimately futile process by which capitalistic nations have been trying to save, invest, and apply to profitable production, a larger proportion of the total income than the technology of industry, taken in conjunction with the conservatism of the arts of consumption, renders possible. It will put the pace of production into a more normal and economical adjustment to the pace of consumption. This will follow from the better or more equal distribution of purchasing power.

The capital and labour of the community will be kept in full and regular employment by a standard of consumption continually rising because no longer artificially depressed. There will not be less saving, but more, and each unit of saving will be more usefully employed. A gradual rise in the normal standard of consumption of the whole community will be substituted for an irregular, unreliable, and insufficient demand for luxuries on the part of the rich. This normal rise of consumption will, acting as an increasing demand for standard articles of production, serve directly and adequately to check that tendency to over-production in great capitalistic enterprises which we have recognised as the premonitory symptom of cyclical depressions, with their stoppage of industry and unemployment.[1]

[1] The explanation of these cyclical expansions and depressions in terms of psychology, as waves of business confidence and distrust expressed through expanding and contracting credit, so popular among

But before quitting this discussion of the supply of capital there are two related issues upon which I ought to touch. One relates to the nature of saving. By common usage saving has been confined to the provision out of income of new forms of material capital. But intelligent foresighted parents have always recognised that they may be doing better for their children by spending any surplus income they possess in giving them a good education than in putting that surplus in the bank. It is fair to add that most economists have endorsed this policy on economic grounds, as one equally serviceable with the other in its future productivity.

But this form of "saving," investment in education and training, has been under-estimated in this country. Far too small a proportion of the nation's surplus income has gone into it. Not only have we been trying to save for national capital a larger proportion of the general income than is useful, or profitable (even in the narrow economic sense), but we have been pursuing this bad and futile course at the cost of the development of the brains and ability of the nation.

This nation is now admittedly handicapped in her industries not by lack of capital or raw labour but by lack of trained ability in the applied sciences, in finance, and in business administration. Though there are other factors in this problem than expenditure on education, the monetary under-valuation of what we may here call brain-capital in favour of material capital has been largely economists, in nowise contravenes the analysis here given. My analysis claims to give a concrete origin for these psychological and credit movements.

responsible for the feebleness of our post-war economic situation. This undervaluation of education is attributable to two causes. The first is the comparative intellectual ease with which the fabric of British capitalism has been built up. Our great business men appear to have got on without trained brains for themselves or the purchase of trained brains in others. The second is the habitual and traditional absorption of the leisure time, energy, interest, and money of all classes in the recreational side of life, a term which includes sport, drink, travel, amusements, and light literature.

A smaller proportion of our aggregate income is needed for the material fabric of capitalism, but a larger proportion for the intellectual fabric of modern industry. This belongs to the problem of reformed distribution of wealth, which is thus seen to be bound up organically and psychologically with enlarged and improved production.

What is wanted by common admission is a larger output of wealth, or income, more equably distributed. Only by a distribution which eliminates surplus can we get into play the incentives necessary to increased and improved productivity. For only thus can we reduce the excessive proportion of income put to business capital, increase the proportion put to intellectual capital, and keep the pressure of consumption high enough to hold taut the sinews of production.

But, it may be said, admitting that the requisite amount of saving can be got in the new Industrial System, what security have we that it will be properly applied? Under the present system skilled financiers are engaged in mobilising the savings of the saving classes and distributing them in various classes of investment in various countries with close expert regard to the risks and yield or productivity of each investment. The knowledge, risk-taking and organising skill, involved in these delicate processes, will be as necessary under the New Order as under the old. But, if large sections of capitalist enterprise are brought under the control of the State which will find the required capital, this delicate work will be entrusted to officials who will have neither the skill nor the incentives requisite to its successful performance.

The issue is of critical importance. For the central Money Power of high finance is the power-house of modern capitalism. It performs a supremely important function in collecting and distributing fluid capital for the feeding of the business organism. The responsibility and the risks attending the work are so great as to require and justify a high rate of payment for it. Take away the larger part of this work and put it into bureaucratic hands, some trades may be starved and others will be glutted for lack of that nice economy of distribution evoked by that conjunction of caution with adventure which marks the successful financier.

Now, admitting the importance of the economical application of savings, I consider this line of criticism fatal to any sudden wholesale transformation of industry and commerce from a profiteering to a public system. But it is less applicable to the limited area of nationalisation here contemplated, and the defects it indicates are there offset by certain positive advantages of public over private finance. The higher qualities of skill and enterprise in the conduct of finance apply to fields of activity which will long remain outside the area of practicable socialism, the development of new industries or new localities, experiments in new processes and the supply of the conveniences and luxuries of life in their later stages of production. In other words, the finance required for our new Industrial Order will be of a more sober and less speculative character which, though involving the same qualities of skill and caution as in the more adventurous departments, involves them in a much lower degree. The problem of economical public finance is, indeed, a serious one, but there is no ground for holding that the use of the borrowing powers of the State to raise and apply productive capital to public enterprises passes the limits of official skill, provided that these enterprises are established businesses engaged in supplying the necessities of the whole community. It would be conformable with the sound principles of representative government to set up a national Finance Council of Industry, upon which should sit elected representatives of the several National Industries, together with representatives of the Treasury, to advise upon the financial requirements of the several public services, the methods of raising the money (by special trade reserves, by taxation or by borrowing), and where a general fund is raised, the

E

apportionment of that fund among the several applicants. To such an advisory Council might also be delegated administrative powers, so as to secure in the several trades the most economical use of the provided capital and the best provisions for payment of the interest and sinking fund out of the annual income. The apportionment of its borrowing powers between the claims of the respective public services, though calling for intelligent skill and discretion, makes no such call upon the higher qualities of financial imagination or calculation as are involved in the opening up of some backward country or the putting of some new speculative process on the market. In the first place, the public capital thus raised will be secured by bonds at fixed interest, and will have the whole credit of the State, i.e., the taxable capacity of the nation, behind it. Secondly, whatever risk still attaches to these new public investments will be sensibly diminished by their variety. This, of course, is an accepted principle of conservative finance from the standpoint of the individual investor, and is equally applicable to the finance of a State, unless it is overborne by the dismal conviction that State control exercises an equally blighting influence upon all sorts of public enterprise.

Those who hold that all capital raised by the State will be unremuneratively employed, in the sense that public management of any sort must be a business failure, will, of course, object that the use of these borrowing powers by the State will be an open drain down which a larger and larger part of the savings of the community will flow, and that the Government will be forced more and more to rely upon increased taxation for the bond-interest which cannot be found out of the income of the public industries. But this is not essentially a financial criticism. It belongs to the central attack upon the New Order because of its inefficiency of management and discipline, a vital issue to which we shall presently direct our close attention.

As regards the financial administration of the public industries, including the provision of the requisite supplies of new capital by the investing public for their improvement and enlargement, no insuperable difficulty, technical or psychological, has been disclosed. The normal incentives to saving will continue to be operative in the New Order, though the savings will be more widely distributed in their sources. Assuming that the other necessary incentives to production operated satisfactorily, the greater security of a decent sub-sistence for the people as a whole would seem to justify the expectation that the required amount of new savings, exposed to less risk and less waste, would be obtainable at a lower rate of interest than was normally necessary under the wasteful system which is passing away. For a large proportion of the present saving is unproductively employed from the social standpoint. Much is employed in maintaining socially wasteful forms of competition, especially in the distributive trades. Much is lost by absorption in enterprises only profitable to those who projected and floated them upon the more gullible classes of investor. But the greatest of all wastes of capital consists in the normal under-employment and the recurrent unemployment of the greater part of the plant and other invested capital of the whole economic community. If a new Industrial Order can eliminate the greater part of these wastes, this economy, by raising the material productivity of invested capital, will lighten the burden of interest as a cost of production and thus enable an increased proportion of the real annual income to be available as the instrument and the incentive of improved efficiency in current efforts of brain and hand labour.

There remains one important branch of the finance of industry and commerce, accounted the most delicate of all, viz., the issue of credit for the financing of individual firms and transactions, and the machinery of discounting and insurance by which this short time credit system is made effective. When it is airily suggested that banking and insurance, the financial power-house of the economic system, may be nationalised, is it contemplated as possible that the existing credit system could be operated even with a moderate measure of success by public officials of some National Bank with branches spread over the country? Can the grant or refusal of an overdraft to a customer, the subscription to an issue of stock, the discounting of a commercial bill, the underwriting of a particular risk—those nice estimates and calculations that are necessary to the working of modern business be left to bureaucrats?

No confident answer to these questions is yet

possible. But they appear to rest upon one chief assumption, viz., that industry and commerce must always remain as risky in their operations as hitherto, i.e., that the same amount of secrecy regarding the financial position of firms, the same amount of ignorance about stocks and prices in the world markets, the same violent and unpredictable changes in the monetary situation must continue. Now if the business world is to be kept as dangerous and as changeful as ever, the case against public control of credit is irrefutable. But may it not be a sound public policy to reduce these risks and regulate these changes? If full obligatory publication of accounts made the financial position of all firms common knowledge, if national and international stocktaking, along the lines of the International Institute of Agriculture, gave reliable information of the present and prospective supplies of leading articles of commerce, and above all, if an international effort were made to stabilise exchanges and to regulate the supplies of currency, might not these risks be confined within such narrow bounds as to make them manageable by National Banks?

But we need not suppose a rapid general advance in this direction. It may well be the case that large and numerous fields of risky finance may still remain, and that Public Banking and Finance will not attempt to interfere with this department of financial risk taking, but will confine itself to the less risky finance of relatively known or calculable business operations.

CHAPTER IV

BRAINS IN INDUSTRY

THE most generally accepted defence of private capitalist enterprise is that it puts brains into industry. Regarded from the standpoint of creative energy both capital and ordinary labour-power are instruments, the productive use of which depends upon the knowledge, intelligence, will, and judgment of certain small groups of superior economic minds, inventors, scientific experts, technical, administrative, commercial, and financial managers. Unless a free flow of such ability is kept in the service of an industry, its successful conduct is insecure, and its springs of progress will dry up. These various orders of ability, from the genius of invention to the more ordinary capacity of the departmental manager, fall under two categories. The former contains the spirit of discovery and adventure, essentially irregular and incalculable in its operation, alternating bouts of strenuous and concentrated energy with periods of torpor. The most primitive forms of industry partook largely of this type of energy, casual out-burst of intense energy directed to some immediate object of food, protection, or other condition of survival, and it remains to-day for many peoples the only tolerable mode of living. The sense of prowess and achievement is an incentive to all work of this order, and sometimes, as in the case of the most laborious and dangerous sports, a sufficient incentive. But creative work, whether in the realm of science or of art, is apt to balk at utilitarian applications. The scientist and the artist require some special inducement if they are to allow their free creative powers to be harnessed to the chariot of industry. Of the inventor, however, it may generally be said, that he has of his free will abandoned this idealist position, and is consciously catering for industry, a sort of middleman between the pure scientist and the business man. But it is generally agreed that industrial progress depends primarily upon free and large supplies of new knowledge from this conjunction of abilities. Nor is it merely a matter of technological advances, improved methods of production through applied chemistry, physics, and biology. On the economic and sociological sides of production a fresh flow of knowledge and experiment into the arts of business administration, management, commerce, and finance, is equally essential to success. Psychology is one of the most neglected streams of economic progress.

If, however, the physical and moral sciences are to be made available for contribution to industrial progress, adequate provisions must be made for directing the creative and inventive ability which flows through them into definitely industrial channels. And this is not the specific function of the inventor, but rather of the higher type of business organiser. For it belongs to this man to keep an eye upon new inventions and new opportunities or other profitable notions and put them into actual use. This is an exceedingly important function, that of the selection of new ideas, schemes, patents, markets, methods, as soon as they reach the level of true business economy. It may be a question of installing a new machine, of taking on some subsidiary process, of establishing a scheme of cost taking, of advising a new share issue, of planning an amalgamation, of opening up a new market. These acts of critical judgment involve high powers of calculation or intuition, the result of which may be an immense economy or expansion of production and a great increase of profits for the firm. Considerable risks of failure must attach to such acts, but the fact of industrial progress attests that they succeed more often than they fail. Indeed, it may be held that industrial progress consists in the performance of such acts.

Making all due allowance for the competitive or the purely predatory character of some of these successful acts, enabling a particular firm to displace and take the trade of its competitors, there remains a great net social gain in the industrial improvements thus brought about. Now in the New Industrial Order it is important to retain as far as possible these methods of progress. And perhaps the gravest charge against the New Order is that it will not make adequate provisions for such ability to function.

BRAINS IN INDUSTRY

" Napoleons of industry, commerce, and finance," it is said, " require a free hand, an unfettered career, and the possibility of immense prizes, to evoke the use of their talents. Withdraw this large personal initiative and these unlimited vistas of personal wealth and power, you paralyse economic progress. Even if you could get your scientist to work for truth's sake and the good of humanity, and if you could furnish suitable rewards for successful inventors, you could not get your great industrials and financiers of industry to do their work in the grey unadventurous world you offer them. Nor is it only these rare and essentially creative talents that are imperilled. The more normal business manager must retain powers of initiative and judgment which seem equally inconsistent with all proposals of industrial democracy and State super-control." Here is Lord Askwith's account of what will commonly be accepted as the proper function and character of an able manager.

" The best managers, while alive to the desires of both employers and men, are as little inclined to submit to official interference of their directors as to factious interference of the employees. I have in mind many such managers whose success in municipal undertakings or private concerns has been due as much to confidence in their power to prevent such interference as to technical knowledge of their business. I imagine the position of such managers when called upon to consult a workman or a committee of their own workmen elected, not because of the ability he or they have shown in the expert business of management, but because a man has succeeded in securing election by his fellows."[1]

The clumsy hand of State ownership and the machinery of representative government in industry will prove fatal to securing the services of these owners of ability!

This is the charge. How is it met? Now, as regards the higher qualities of technical and administrative invention, it may be contended that there will normally be less scope for their service in the national industries than in those left to private enterprise. For the former are selected on the basis of the greater regularity of their production and demand and the well-established methods they employ. In the main the goods and services they give out are standardised and the processes are relatively routine. There will, therefore, be less call upon the inventive and experimental in improvements of technique and business method, while the abilities which go to the discovery and development of new markets, by tapping either new local areas or new strata of human wants, will be less important than in the more plastic industries that remain in private hands. The same qualifying circumstances will apply also to the ordinary managerial work. The elements of initiative, critical judgment, enterprise, will be far less conspicuous in industries which have passed through a long competitive career and have anchored in the haven of some huge combination. Such businesses are properly held " ripe " for nationalisa-

[1] " Industrial Problems and Disputes," p. 476.

tion, having largely shed those activities and virtues which appertain to competitive trade.

In order to justify the nationalisation of such industries it is not necessary, therefore, to prove that they preserve intact all the flexibility and power of growth which belong to youth. Indeed, so far as it is reasonable to regard the fund of creative and adventurous energy equipped for industry as of limited amount, it is evidently a true social economy in its use that the greater part should be applied to the younger, more plastic industries which remain under private capitalism, where it will be more productively employed. To divert great inventive or business talent from the new rising occupations into State industries would be a false social economy. The more ordinary kinds of ability and mental efficiency conducive to reliable conservative administration will be relatively far more important in this class than in the other.

It is doubtless possible to overstress this contrast between older established and conservative businesses and the newer and more progressive ones. The stiff opposition in the former to the acceptance of new ideas and the adoption of new disturbing methods is a grave defect. The very size and fundamental importance of such industries as railways, mining, insurance, may be interpreted as giving a greater not a less social value to the qualities of high adventurous ability that can effect some radical reform of structure or of working. Certain grave wastes or other defects, discernible in what we term the great routine services, whether publicly or privately administered, appear to testify to an insufficiency of high creative and executive ability in the control. Great bodies move slowly, but it is of the utmost importance they should be kept moving, for each step in progress that they make is fraught with larger social gain than fifty steps of corresponding size and novelty in minor industries.

This means that every care should be taken to attract into and retain in these public services a requisite amount of high ability and initiative. But it still remains true that the proportionate part played by these qualities is smaller than in those more plastic industries where much more numerous and various changes are continually required.

It is, therefore, no sufficient ground for condemning a national system of railways or of telegraphs that it does not bring into its employment and evoke the amount of pushful energy and enterprise found even in these very industries under private enterprise conducted under different developmental conditions. It may be true that a private postal service (were it to remain competitive—an unlikely hypothesis) would be more flexibly responsive to public demands and might give to some parts of its customers better service for less money. But these gains would be at the expense of a loss of security and uniformity, and perhaps by taking away some business talent more advantageously employed in other fields of business enterprise. In other words, these qualities of security and uniformity, essential in certain industries to an orderly civilisation, are cheaply purchased by the surrender of other qualities of alertness and flexibility which are relatively less important in these particular industries and are inherently inconsistent with the former qualities. Well-established trades, supplying regular wants by standardised methods, do not require the same orders of ability as do younger and more experimental trades. It is as idle to charge them with slowness and inadaptiveness as it is to bring the same charge against politicians or business men. Each class of man or business has the defects of his qualities, and the qualities of his defects. Admitted that the absence of the speculative career, with its big prizes and many blanks, fails to attract certain types of masterful initiative and makes for conservatism, is that any damage to the social economy?

This type of business is properly conservative, and the type of ability which shuns it is better employed in more inherently adventurous occupations. The same fault has been found with joint stock enterprise as compared with individual businesses, the limited stake of each investor entailing a proportionate weakening in his incentive to maintain efficiency and promote progressive methods. The specific charge cannot be rebutted, but there remains the adequate reply that this weakening of personal incentive is the necessary price paid for the great economy of large-scale production in many branches of our capitalist system.

But, though it is far less important to have a free flow of creative, inventive, and initiative ability in the public services than in private enterprise, it would be foolish to contend that society can dispense with such qualities even in the most conservative type of service. Modern science is continually putting up new propositions to the business world, and though the experimental tests are usually best left to private enterprise, there remains the vitally important task of claiming these fruits of service for the public welfare. Is it inevitable that the public services should remain incapable of seeing and adapting to the public use new profitable notions?

Officialism, we are told, is necessarily obstructive to new ideas and the acquisition of new habits, and the suggestion is that the managers of private enterprise are constantly alert for their acceptance.

Now, before dealing with the charge of official obstructiveness, let us consider for a moment the validity of this view of private enterprise in those great British industries which come within the range of the nationalising proposals.

How far, for example, is it true that the directors, managers, and shareholders of our railways and coal mines have shown themselves so keenly alive to the interests of their shareholders that they have missed few opportunities of adopting the new technical and business methods which expert science has discovered in this and other countries? Take first the shareholders whose profits are supposed to furnish the prime incentive to efficiency and economy. Do they keep a keen lookout for the technical advances which will improve their investments, and through the directorate they elect force these improvements upon the management? Everybody knows that they neither do nor can perform this function. Their real power even to appoint their directorate is, save in rare moments of upheaval, nugatory; their power to initiate technical or administrative reforms is simply nil. Their situation remains to-day as it was when Adam Smith wrote " The greater part of the proprietors seldom pretend to understand anything of the business of the company . . . give themselves no trouble about it, but receive contentedly each half-yearly or yearly dividend as the directors think proper to make to them." Yet when these words were written the liability of " proprietors " was unlimited. Now that it is limited to the amount of their shares, their incentive to understand and to promote their profitable interests is considerably less. But as regards many of our great industries, in particular our railways, Adam Smith's language would apply with slight qualification to the directorates. What proportion of the 1,200 railway directors in this country has by training or experience acquired any expert knowledge of railroading? How many directors of our 1,500 colliery companies have any expert knowledge of mining? The huge waste of efficiency in these two fundamental industries, attributable to the ignorance or slackness of the supreme control, has been quite recently attested by impartial commissions. A practical measure of business inefficiency in one crucial instance, the use of our wasting material asset, coal, is afforded in a recent article[1] by one of our leading mining

[1] *Manchester Guardian Commercial*, May 19th, 1921.

experts, Mr David Brownlie, who writes: " I have been associated with the complete testing of nearly 500 coal-fired boiler plants and the inspection of nearly 2,000 plants, and the net working efficiency actually varies from 32—82$\frac{1}{2}$ per cent, the true average being about 60 per cent. . . . It should not be forgotten that we have squandered our coal in the most reckless manner in the past, and that we are still wasting it to-day in millions of tons. By adopting reasonable and intelligent methods we can save 50,000,000 tons of coal per annum out of our present consumption of 190,000,000 tons." This estimate is supported by the Coal Conservative's Sub-committee in its Interim Report on Electric Power Supply.[1] " If Power supply in the United Kingdom were dealt with on comprehensive lines and advantage taken of the most modern engineering developments, the saving of coal throughout the whole country would, in the near future, amount to 55,000,000 tons per annum on the present output of manufactured products." In the recent Report of an inquiry into the Steel and Iron Industry by the Industrial Fatigue Research Board the waste from refusal to apply known methods of economy is thus summarised: " It seems probable that if all the iron and steel works in this country adopted the most efficient methods, they could, on an average, improve their output by something between 50 and 100 per cent."[2]

[1] Cd. 8880, p. 5.
[2] Industrial Fatigue Research Board Report 5, p. 95.

BRAINS IN INDUSTRY

Even when we take the directly responsible employer, whether managing director or salaried manager, in these or other developed branches of great industry, where it might be presumed that the capitalist incentive of private profit would work with the greatest intensity, the result is very disappointing. Steady administration and competent routine, careful judgment on minor issues of lines of goods or factory discipline—yes. But quick apprehension of the new contributions which chemistry and physics are continually offering to our directly utilisable knowledge, faith in scientific research, willingness to experiment in new business methods, these are exceedingly rare qualities among our great industrialists.

Though every great modern business bristles with problems of high intellectual as well as practical moment, physical, financial, and administrative, how many responsible heads of business in this country possess any expert training in mechanics, finance, economics, or psychology? The very notion of the need of such training appears to almost all of them a ridiculous pandering to an intellectualism which unfits men for a real business life. Though a few of them are intelligent enough to recognise that Germany has got ahead of us in some profitable trades by employing scientific experts, and that the higher business training of young Americans is consistent with a rapid lucrative career, very little has been done to secure for our industries these fruits of expert thinking and training. Here is a costly, perhaps disastrous, failure of the profiteering motive

F

in our employing class. They have not put brains into business, they have not been quick to catch hold of new profitable ideas and to scrap outworn methods. Energy and industry many of them possess, but it is very wastefully employed because of their contemptuous scepticism of science and all that science stands for in adapting nature to the needs of man. Nor is that all. Many responsible employers have neither energy nor industry in the measure that their fathers had. They are not intensely interested in business, it does not come first with them, as with the builders of our great industries: they are gentlemen, sportsmen, clubmen, social frivolers, to an extent which was not true even of the late Victorian masters. They value their business not as their fathers did, or as the typical American or German employer still does, as a great career, but as a necessary instrument to serve their more enjoyable functions.

It is distinctly humorous to hear these inexpert and slovenly-minded directors and employers denouncing in their clubs, or on their ever-lengthening weekend holidays, the refusal of their workers to give a fair day's work for a fair day's wage.

But, it may be urged, granting that employers are slow to recognise the uses of science and of expert business training, public control and management, whether by a body of permanent State officials or by representative committees, will be still less responsive to new ideas and improved methods. I am not opening here the whole question of business competence, but only the attitude towards those high qualities of intelligence and judgment upon which the success of a great modern progressive business so largely depends. If the incentive of great personal gain under private enterprise proves so inadequate for the evocation of these high qualities, how will they fare when this incentive is removed? The sterilising influence of a bureaucracy upon the seeds of progress has passed into a byword. No official, it is said, will undertake the risk or responsibility of those experiments which are necessary to vitality and growth, or even adopt approved reforms which disturb the even tenor of office routine. As for representative Committees, either they will harden into officialism, if, as is almost inevitable, they are led to repose their confidence in a permanent executive staff, or they may lapse into the equally injurious extreme of a too facile experimentalism, or they may even alternate between these two defects.

But before deciding what remedy, if any, exists, let us look a little closer into this malady of officialism. Officials will not take responsibility or run risks, because they are not obliged to do so by the terms on which they hold office. Under private enterprise officials who do not " make good " to the satisfaction of directors have got to go. A directorate, however self-elected, which loses too much of the subscribed capital or lets down too rapidly the dividend, has got to go. Public officials, however, here, and in most countries, enjoy a great security of tenure. They may waste the public money, many let down the industry or service entrusted to their care, but the persons, who have the formal power to dismiss them, are not themselves the losers, and have no sufficient incentive to take this drastic step. Even were they disposed to a purging of the staff, they would find great difficulty in fastening upon any individuals the personal delinquencies which it is the interest of official staffs to hide. Elected representatives, whether on a Parliamentary Committee or on an Industrial Committee, can in effect do very little to check the incompetence or slackness of the permanent official. Still less can they insure those processes of selection, rejection, and stimulation, by which the ablest employers get the finest work out of the best men in their employ.

Now, it is possible, while admitting the general truth of these damaging charges, to mitigate their effect, by making bureaucratic control itself more intelligent, and more responsive to the demands of progressive industry. In his examination before the Committee on the Coal Industry Lord Haldane made an interesting excursion into this psychological field. Fully recognising the deficiencies of the Civil Service and Ministerial Control as exercised at present, he indicates lines of reformation, drawn in part from the Army and Navy, in part from private enterprise. The " system " of the Civil Service is hostile to initiative. " That is where the business man has the strength and the advantage. He is in an atmosphere of initiative. The Civil Service is not in an atmosphere of initiative. The soldier and the sailor to a large extent are."[1] There exists to-day " a large class

---

[1] " The Problem of Nationalisation," p. 28.

of men who combine the strongest sense of public duty with the greatest energy and capacity for initiative." This source of productivity is largely wasted. Of the Army and Navy he says, " You pick a man because he is particularly good at the sort of work you want him for. You ask him to devote himself to administration, and, if he does, you may get a man just as valuable and just as good as you will find in the business world. It is quite true he has not got what is the great impulse in the business world, namely, the desire to make a fortune for himself, but he has another motive, which, in my experience, is equally potent with the best class of men, namely, the desire to distinguish himself in the service of the State."

Now granted that we have in this desire for distinction in the Army a real incentive to efficiency and in particular to initiative, can we graft it on a public industry with sufficient efficacy? Distinction is directly associated with such orders of personal achievement as rouse the public admiration and respect. It may be taken for granted that most forms of military achievement have a stronger and quicker response than could be got from any action of equal skill and value in the field of industry or commerce. But, it may be replied, we are not concerned chiefly with popular appreciation in the wider sense, but with such professional distinction as comes to a soldier from his purely administrative work. A good deal could be done within the service to encourage the motive of distinction. At present a positive secretiveness prevails, a hiding away of the very name of a public servant who has done great meritorious work. " I think there are a great many men who would be prepared to serve the State at moderate salaries, if they were to have the prospect of becoming distinguished in the sense of having rank and recognition." It is not easy to separate what may be designated the legitimate selfishness of such an appeal from that devotion to the public service which it engenders and nourishes. The main practical issue is, however, best set forth in the following question and answer. Sir Adam Nimmo: " Do you think you can draw a real comparison between your ability to secure special men for the Army and Navy and special men for the ordinary working of an industry? The point I have in mind is this—' Do not men go into the Army and the Navy really for special reasons, under special motives, which would not apply, in the same sense, to an ordinary industry?'—Yes, but I want them to apply to an ordinary industry. I want to make the service of the State in civilian things as proud a position as it is with the Army and Navy to-day, and for these to be public spirit, public honour, and public recognition. Just as you get an engineer officer who will throw a bridge over a river, with extraordinary skill, although he seems to have no materials with which to do it, so you may develop the same kind of capacity in that officer when he deals with a civilian problem."

BRAINS IN INDUSTRY

Lord Haldane raises an issue of tremendous importance when he avers " There exists to-day a large class of men who combine the strongest sense of public duty with the greatest energy and capacity for initiative." For the common assumption has always been that initiative is closely linked with purely personal aims and feelings, at any rate in the business world. Modern competition in England, and elsewhere, was built up by hard pushful gain-seeking personalities whose selfish aims were simple and avowed, and it has been assumed that the prospect of great wealth and power alone can evoke the resourceful energy and determined will needed for a great business enterprise.

An attempt to displace these men in the command of industry by public servants, however carefully selected, will, it is claimed, spell disaster. The " large class " of which Lord Haldane speaks, does not exist ! The Army may be able to draw a tolerable handful of public-spirited men with initiative, but they will not rally to the call of industry !

Now, no confident reply can be made to this objection. So much depends on education, so much upon reform in public service. Our national services comprise so little in the nature of directly productive industry as to furnish a poor test. Our municipal services afford a better one. I think it will be admitted that many managers of most municipal undertakings are by no means lacking either in public spirit or in initiative. So far as the charge of lack of enterprise so commonly brought against gas-and-water socialism has any validity, it is due less to official slackness or incompetence than to the ignorance, suspicion and timidity, of a Committee and a Council with the fear of the ratepayer continually before them. If managers and directors of private companies prove to be more enterprising and progressive in their business methods (a much-debated issue which lies outside my present scope) this superiority can be attributed chiefly to the more enlightened control of their directorate. This statement does not conflict with the strictures passed above upon the low average standard of expert knowledge possessed by most directors. The standard of a municipal committee will as a rule be definitely lower, their personnel more shifting, their attendance less regular, and the average ratepayer from whom their financial resources are drawn is more ignorant and blinder to his true interests as a citizen than is the average shareholder to his interest as dividend receiver. There is little to be said in defence of the efficiency of the existing form of municipal democracy, except that it is a marvel that it should secure so relatively high a standard of municipal service. But this larger issue is not relevant to a discussion of the quality of initiative in public officials.

My point is that under such conditions lack of initiative and enterprise cannot be charged against the heads of municipal undertakings. There is no evidence that they are lacking in these high qualities, though it may be admitted that the conditions under which they work are such as may deter certain types of high-spirited and adventurous men from embarking upon these official careers.

It does not, however, seem desirable to press the analogy of military service as far as Lord Haldane inclines to do. The appeal to the spirit of personal exploit cannot be made on the same level. Business adventure is intrinsically less simple in its appeal to the primary emotions than is military adventure, even under the conditions of modern machine-warfare. The glory of a serviceable industrial coup cannot be made to equal that of a successful military coup. To pretend that it can is injurious sentimentalism. It is a different sort of initiative and adventure that is wanted. The man of business brings to his civilian problem possibly the same blend of calculation and intuition as goes into an act of military initiative, but he is seldom justified in taking such high risks, for failure or success seldom counts so high. The difference reposes ultimately upon the directly vital significance of the two acts. A soldier whose bold initiative saves or loses the lives of an army and perhaps the freedom of a nation has incentives which cannot apply to the initiative of an industrial official which achieves a notable economy of fuel or some other gain that finds its human expression in a reduction of the rates.

With such qualification, however, I would accept as reasonable Lord Haldane's opinion that plenty of public-spirited men with initiative are available, provided we look for them and supply them with such opportunities of public recognition as give dignity to a career. It is largely a matter of spreading our net widely in the way of education and selection. So long as only one in ten of our families is able or willing to avail itself of such opportunities of higher education as exist, while that education itself is very ill-adapted to discover and encourage the types of live intelligence which are needed, no large crop of public-spirited initiative is likely to be at our disposal for the public services. Hitherto the higher professions have been the preserves of a small fraction of our upper and middle classes, with a thin precarious trickle of boys coming up from that section of the working class families able and willing to give a chance to a child of exceptional ability to win school prizes. It is not merely more equality of educational opportunity, but better education that is wanted, that is, education consciously and skilfully directed to the discovery of the personal aptitudes that give distinction to a human being, and to such training as will make these aptitudes socially serviceable through an assured career. Initiative, in itself, is almost meaningless for our purpose, hardly distinguishable from the quality called push. In order to be socially serviceable it must be harnessed to some particular talent or quality of intelligence. If what we are after is securing for the public services men and women with the insight, the courage and the energy, to seize the opportunities which the flowing tide of knowledge place within their reach and work them for the public good, we must reform the processes of selection which supply these men and women to the services at the same time as we endeavour to de-mechanise the services themselves.

But when all is said and done, it may be true that high genius, great adventure, supreme initiative, will not be coupled with such public spirit as will induce their owners to place their gifts at the direct disposal of the community. It may well be that a passionate sense of personal freedom, or such egoism as attaches commonly to what we term the artistic temperament, will prevent the public services getting so large a proportion of these talents as are found in private business ventures. Immense self-confidence will shun the necessary shackles of any service. The office of a trust or great combination fails to attract a certain vigorous type of business man who prefers a riskier and less profitable career " upon his own." This brings me back to the reflection that in a social life such as we are contemplating, where only certain essential and relatively routine industries are socialised, there will be a net economy in leaving a larger share of creative intelligence and initiative to private enterprise, because, though useful in either sphere, it is more useful in the latter.

If this appears to anyone a surrender to private profiteering, I would reply that such objection rests upon a misapprehension of our reasonable attitude towards private enterprise. Our limited socialism is defended on the ground that the elimination of private profit as the directing incentive of industry is so difficult an achievement, politically and economically, that it is best confined to those industries which are of fundamental importance to the national life and from which the safeguard of competition has already been withdrawn. This means that we regard private enterprise in non-essential trades as relatively innocuous, partly, because profiteering in them is more evocative of improvements in the arts of production than in the older and more fundamental trades, partly because the keen competition which there survives continues to secure to the community of consumers a large share in the gains of their efficiency. It is, in other words, a sound public economy to encourage a high output of energy, enterprise, initiative and risk-taking, in these non-essential industries by offering high prizes for conspicuous success. The prizes may sometimes be extravagantly high, and taxation may adjust them to a nicer social economy of incentives. But we are not out to deny that certain orders of high personal efficiency are probably associated with a selfish materialism which makes it socially desirable to give large financial rewards as a necessary condition of getting these highly productive services. When it can be shown that fuller recognition, or the essential interest of a successful career, will dispense with the profiteering motive, why then these industries are ripe for social services. Until then we shall do wisely to leave them as the proper field or hunting-ground of a certain type of masterful business man able to put immense personal energy, initiative, and skill into his business on condition that he runs it for his own gainful end. This, of course, is said without prejudice to the right and duty of the community to protect his employees against any oppressive or socially injurious terms of employment he may be able to impose, or the consuming public against any socially injurious terms he imposes for his services.

The challenge to our new Industrial Order upon the score of failure of initiative and enterprise in its administration is, therefore, not so convincing as it sounds. It is met partly by admission. It is admitted that a certain selfish or predatory type of business man, exceedingly successful in the sphere of private enterprise by his ability, persistent energy and audacity, is not likely to put these qualities at the service of the community. Let it be granted that a Rockefeller or a Leverhulme will not " function " in our socialised industry. What then? These men, you say, are great constructive geniuses and we cannot afford to lose them for society. Well, it is not necessary to lose them. If their present free masterful operations, though motived primarily by desire for personal power or gain, carry rich incidental fruits for humanity, it may be best to leave to them this sphere of industry, gathering and harvesting for humanity as much as possible of these individual gains. Let them dominate the non-essential industries, organise them and make what money they can out of them, subject to taxation and public protection of employees and consumers.

It is not indispensable to social industry to tame and harness to the public service this sort of leviathan. He would not work in social harness, but would prove a plunger and a wrecker. Social industry, moreover, does not need him, though it would gladly utilise some of his capacities, if they could be divorced from others with which, however, they are inseparably bound. The real point is whether the social industries can attract, employ, and retain other men of initiative, ability, and enterprise, adequate to the needs of businesses no longer in their early experimental stage but developed into full grown organisms, which, though capable of progress and improvement, are relatively staid and conservative in their operation. Faguet[1] and other critics of officialism make it a chief complaint that public services confine their appeal to over-cautious timid natures who shun the bracing atmosphere of the battle of life and play for safety. And it may well be admitted that there is this danger of a feeding of the public services with safe men. But, after all, the first aim of organised society is safety. Progress, it is conceded, must come chiefly out of the less organised, the more free elements. Provided we can get into our new Social Order a sufficiency of initiative and enterprise, we should do well to entrust the main body of these services to men whose nature is fitted to essentially conservative employment.

If it be replied that these conservative natures tend to slackness and obstruction and get in the way of our men of initiative, our reply is an admission that over-security attaches to the tenure of office in most public services, but that the vice of bureaucracy is not chargeable in the same degree to the representative government which we premise.

[1] *Cf.* " The Dread of Responsibility " (Putnam & Sons).

It ought, in other words, to be possible to get into these public services a full sufficiency of resourceful and progressive minds, and to afford them sufficient scope for their qualities with public recognition and distinction as personal incentives in substitution for the higher pecuniary prizes of success in private enterprises.

Probably we should not get into the public service Napoleons of commerce and finance. We do not want them. There is a type of business genius in which the predatory quality devours the creative. Mr Tawney well indicates this truth in citing as the central feature in recent economic evolution " the bifurcation of industry and finance."¹ For the predatory species, the Napoleon, is essentially financier, exercising his skill and powers in financial coups. Often he takes his origin, and finds his financial legs, in some big concrete line of business, appearing as an organising genius in oil, real estate, mining, shipping, or railroads. But self-interest, opportunity, and the spirit of adventure, drive him rapidly to widen his field of enterprise, taking in other lines of business which impinge upon, overlap, or substitutionally compete with, his first line. He starts by organising oil, but soon finds that gas and electricity, as illuminants, are within his sphere of interest, that oil tanks bring him into close business relations with rails and shipping, and that banking and insurance are not really alien propositions. By horizontal or vertical contacts the specialised business man thus passes by an

¹ " The Acquisitive Society," Ch. VII.

inevitable process into the generalised business man, i.e., the financier who realises and utilises money-power freely over the business world. From a trust or control or combine in shipping, coal and steel, electric plant, or street railways, it is natural for your Stinnes, Ellerman, or Rockefeller, to develop free pecuniary resources for utilisation outside this special field, for a business life of exploit in the adventurous atmosphere of the stock exchange, or of banking as practised in America and Germany and to a growing extent in this country. Now the general financier is one who utilises other people's money for his own private profit, using his own money, partly, indeed, as a contributory fund, but mainly as a bait and a guarantee. His position enables him to gather in a large part of the real savings of the community, and to direct them into the several channels, commercial and territorial, where they can be employed most profitably, first from the standpoint of the financier, secondly, from that of his clients or investors, thirdly, from that of the community of business men, workers, and consumers. The defenders of this system will contend (along the old lines of Adam Smith's " led as by an invisible hand ") that the gain of the financier is linked inseparably with gains to the investor and the community, and that in this sense the financier is a servant of the public, using his skill and knowledge to distribute the available free capital in the best possible manner. So, likewise, they will represent his operations in the stock exchanges as a process of readjusting values which is necessary in order to keep capital properly apportioned to its most advantageous uses. Every financial operation, including the elaborate speculations in futures, is defended on this same ground, the theory being that they are the machinery by which ultimately the productive capital and labour of a country (or the world at large) are most usefully employed. Now this is a very false rendering of the facts. Even in concrete businesses abuses of finance are increasingly prevalent. In mining or railway companies it is common enough for the present financial interests of directors or shareholders to impose a working policy, which is wasteful in the long run and crippling to technical efficiency. To secure immediate profit or keep up dividends, the directors of a mine may " cream the pit," the directors of a railway let down its rolling stock. Sometimes this is done in ignorance, but more often it indicates a genuine conflict of interest between the present holders of certain stocks and shares and the future holders. To over-estimate the value of a failing business so as to clear out of it advantageously, is a common proceeding.

Another definitely anti-social employment of financial ability and resource is in those processes of forced absorption and organisation upon a basis of enlarged share capital by which the economies of combination and the anticipatory gains of monopoly are taken out beforehand by the financial organisers of a great business structure. This process frequently involves a plundering of the weaker competitors, forced into a combine upon terms dictated by their financial masters, and often

G

123

a weakening of the business structure which emerges, by reason of the over-capitalisation to which it has been subjected in the interest of men who have no permanent stake in the industry. Behind all lies the fleecing of the consumer by high prices rendered possible by combination and rendered necessary in order to remunerate upon a " reasonable level " the highly watered capital.

But the deepest-seated peril of the money-power consists in the dependence of its profitable operation upon insecurity of investments. The deliberately planned fluctuations of values on the money, stock, and produce markets, are the sources of the largest, most numerous, and most immediately lucrative financial operations. Now, though there is a legitimate field for skilled finance in the direction and adjustment of capital values, the financial interest in insecurity, this rocking of markets, in order to get profit from the rise and fall, is a grave anti-social operation. And what is probably worse, there is no clear line of demarcation between the legitimate and socially useful and the illegitimate and socially injurious functions of finance.

The type of business man who works in this adventurous atmosphere has initiative, courage, insight, and sometimes genius. He is often perhaps truly regarded as a necessary factor in the modern world of finance. But that is not his vindication, but rather the condemnation of a financial system which requires and evokes his predatory presence. Such useful service as he renders, incidental to his profiteering office, he is overpaid for. Most of his work is socially noxious, and only seems necessary in an era properly described as one of financial anarchy. The most disturbed conditions of political and economic society are the most advantageous for him, because he gets his handsome living out of the big fluctuations of values which then occur. Thus he is the enemy of social order, and a far more dangerous one than the political anarchist or the labour agitator whom it is his wont to denounce but from whose activities he reaps no inconsiderable portion of his profits.

The charge against the new Industrial Order that it will be lacking in initiative and enterprise is, therefore, met by the following considerations :

1. The industries proposed for nationalisation, being relatively stable and routine in character, have less use for these qualities than those industries which remain within the sphere of private competitive enterprise.

2. A great deal of this initiative and enterprise has no rightful place in socialised industry, being directed either to the achievement of profitable victories over trade competitors, or to the establishment of a monopolistic power to tax consumers, or to the performance of successful coups in the financial sphere.

3. Nationalised industries should, however, be able to attract as much of these creative and progressive qualities as they require from men who combine them with a keen public spirit and a high regard for such distinction as the public services can be made to afford.

CHAPTER V

INCENTIVES TO THE EFFICIENCY OF LABOUR

BUT will not a socialised industry lead to slack discipline, less efficient work, and reduced productivity on the part of the employees? This fear of what is called " the government stroke," definitely slower and less vigorous than the outside business stroke, is everywhere a chief obstacle to the acceptance of nationalisation or municipalisation. Is it not a fact that in government offices work is put through more slowly than in ordinary business firms? Is not the cost of production in public workshops generally higher than in private ones? Is there not a tendency to take on more men for a municipal job than a private firm would employ, and to spin it out longer? Is there not a good deal of jobbery and political pull in the engagement of men, and a slowness in getting rid of inefficient workers and officials?

It is idle to deny that these charges are substantially true of most public services. Nor are they adequately met by allusions to the driving and speeding habits of private employers for forcing an excessive output of energy out of their employees. No doubt some allowance should rightly be made for the social and human stand-point of the public employer. It is not his interest to overwork and wear out prematurely his workers, or even to dismiss them on light grounds. For he recognises that he will have to keep them and their families if they are broken down or out of work, whereas the private employer has no such obligations. But while this consideration may reasonably affect the conditions both of work and of pay favourably to the public employee, it cannot warrant the slackness and the slowness prevalent in many public services.

The very genuine foreboding lest nationalisation of mines and railways would lead to permanent subsidisation of these industries out of other industries, in order that these classes of public employees may receive more money for an easier day's work than prevails in other less favoured industries, must be plainly confronted. It proceeds from the belief that in these socialised industries no adequate incentive will be brought to bear, either directly upon the ordinary rank and file to evoke their energetic work, or upon the managers and overseers, to secure a fair output, because of the belief that any deficit can and will be made up out of the public purse. It is evident that this charge is not unrelated to that charge of lack of initiative and enterprise which we have already explored in the higher region of officialism. The consciousness of holding a safe, soft, and well-paid job means slow work and slack discipline.

Now it must be admitted at once that, unless socialised industries can preserve a measure of efficiency and productivity not much below that of private enterprise, they are not merely undesirable but impossible. For though the tax-payer may find the funds to meet an occasional deficit in the accounts of the one or two existing industries conducted by the State, such as the Post Office, it cannot continue to subsidise heavily a number of great industries like coal-mining and railroads. There can, therefore, be no case for the larger policy of nationalisation unless there is a reasonable probability of such efficiency as will enable these industries to pay their way. Since unity of organisation and management may be expected to achieve considerable economies as compared with multiplicity and competition, some margin may be forthcoming to meet a slightly higher wage-bill under national ownership. But no considerable let-down of personal energy and productivity is practicable.

There are those who will treat this admission as obviously fatal to the cause of nationalisation. That is, however, only the case if it be assumed that public ownership precludes any form of effective management. Now this assumption is clearly unwarranted. It would be possible for the State, after acquiring ownership over the mines and railways, to lease them out to private companies upon terms which would leave the previous incentives to efficiency among the employees virtually unimpaired. This, however, is not the problem which confronts us. For we have assumed that the new Industrial Order requires the substitution of some representative government for autocracy in the socialised industries. Within this scheme of government must then be found or devised motives adequate to evoke from the wills of workers in mines, workshops, railways, offices, productive energy at least as high as they have hitherto yielded to the economic pressures brought to bear on them in private employ. I say, at least as high, for it is common knowledge that the weak financial condition of the mining and the railway industries is in part attributable to the growing reluctance of workers to work as hard as they used to do for companies they regard as profiteers. It is no sufficient answer to point out that railway shareholders have for a long time past been getting a very low return upon their capital, and that in normal times this would probably be true of most owners of mining shares. The war has helped to ripen a state of mind among the " conscious minority " of organised labour, that is in active revolt against working for " capitalists." It is not possible to estimate how wide-spread and intense this revolutionary consciousness has become. Except in a few spots it is probably confined to little knots of socialists, communists or syndicalists, committed in theory and policy to the destruction of the capitalist system. But though this minority is far from negligible, on account of its active leadership and influence at certain moments over the more vague but susceptible mind of the majority, its importance as a determinant economic factor in this country is greatly over-rated by conservatives. The imputation of Bolshevism, or Socialism, to the mass of organised

workers is a rhetorical invention of " improperty."[1]
On the other hand, the notion that the working
classes can be got back into their normal pre-war
acquiescence in the wage system is equally false.
War experience and war-time visions have had
their withering effect on custom. The unrest,
which was gathering with the new century, and
its hold-up of the progress of the working classes,
have been converted into a more active brew of
discontent. This, doubtless, might have been
allayed and retarded by wage and hour concessions, had the industrial situation permitted. But
post-war prices, taxation, and depressed trade,
have made such alleviation impossible. So discontent passes into something like revolt, a grop-
ing demand for some transformation of the system
which shall give the workers a solid stake in
industry and some voice in the control of it.

The reality and persistence of this unrest, discontent, revolt, however, are not understood unless
we take account of the new knowledge, the town
contacts, travel, reading, the cinema, which by
opening up wider interests in life have been rous-
ing everywhere a revulsion against the drabness,
monotony, and mechanical grind of the ordinary
working day, not to be doped by some shortening
of hours and a few more holidays. Education in
the formal sense contributed not much to this state
of mind, except among the active-minded few; but
these looser social impacts have profoundly affected

[1] For the signification and justification of this term I
may refer readers to my book, " Democracy after the
War " (Allen & Unwin).

the temper of the working classes. The fact that they do not know exactly what they want, or how to formulate it, is not material. The point is that this growing dissatisfaction with economic conditions, taken in conjunction with some loosely conceived economic notions about profiteering and the limited demand for labour, has brought about a more or less conscious or, at any rate, habitual restriction of output in many trades, especially in those where, like building, machinery is not there to set the pace, and where piece-rates are not in vogue.

The policy of " ca canny " may be easily exposed for its economic fallacies by theorists, but the short view, natural to most workers concerned only with the here and now of a particular local labour-market, gives a sort of reasonable sanction to their general resentment and suspicion about exploitation. In their present shapelessness their demands cannot be designated Socialism or any other " ism." Indeed, so far as the great majority of workers are concerned, it is doubtful whether they consciously recognise that they are out for anything except wages, hours, and security against unemployment. But it is well for us to recognise that under the new circumstances in which we live, these concrete demands cannot be satisfied without something like a transformation of our economic system. And in the transformed system all classes of labour, mental and manual, must have a recognised place and voice.

The word " status " has conveniently asserted itself as descriptive of the want. It might mean anything from recognition of the Union to an equal voice with the employer in the management. Indeed, it must evidently mean different things in different industries. Its minimum actual significance, however, is a demand that labour shall have a " real " or perhaps an " equal " voice with " capital " in determining the conditions of employment of labour. This, however, means something more than wage and hours' contracts. It includes questions of the use of machinery, dilution, workshop discipline, and provisions against unemployment, and involves the establishment of some regular and representative body in the workshop and the trade for operating this " status."

A further " status " seeks, by workshop committees and otherwise, to " take over " a larger amount of discipline, as to modes of employment and dismissal and detailed regulations of the conditions under which work is done, ousting the manager and overseer from a part of his " control." The logic of this movement drives towards an equal participation of labour in all managerial functions which relate to the actual operations of the factory, workshop, mine, or other plant, leaving to the employer the buying and selling processes, the general finance and book-keeping, and the determination of the sorts and quantities of goods which are to be made.

The Whitley Council and its Workshop Committees are an experiment on this level, based on a belief that labour will be satisfied with an " equal voice " in all matters " directly " affecting conditions of labour, and will leave the employer's other functions intact, including his right to make whatever profits he can under the new circumstances of restricted control. It may well be the case that for the present, at any rate, the demand for status may be satisfied in some industries by these Councils, or by the Trade Boards which are their substitute in less organised industries. But it is likely that experience of their methods will bring out ever more clearly the falsehood of the assumption that the interests of capital and labour are wrought into full harmony by any scheme which leaves the ultimate control of the industry and the profits to the employer. The success of the Whitley Council presumes a complete organisation both of employers and employees fixing standard wages, hours, and other expenses of production, and leading by a natural process to co-operation and combination in the purchase of materials and in the sale of the product, including price-agreements and apportionment of the market. Now, leaving aside for the present all consideration of the relations of these combinations or cartels to the consumer, it is pretty evident that, partly by economies of production and competition, partly by control of market, they are likely to be able to earn surplus profits to a share of which the representatives of labour will assuredly assert their claim.

If peace is to be maintained, it will be bought by profit-sharing, which must, therefore, be regarded as a next stage in the evolution of a new " status " for labour. Now such profit-sharing differs from that commonly in vogue, inasmuch as it aims at the participation of labour in the surplus profits of monopoly, not merely the sharing of a gain attributable to the greater care or efficiency of labour.

Leaving, however, for later discussion this attempted harmony of capital and labour by profit-sharing, let us turn to a further and a bolder extension of labour "status." To get rid of "the domination of capital" has long been the cherished idea of revolutionary labour. But it has generally conceived some forcible expropriation of the ownership of capital as necessary. Experiments in co-operative business, however, point another way. Why should not the workers in a business themselves own the capital? That, however, is only possible where the capital required per worker is small, or when the workers are so exceptionally well off as to amass some considerable savings. This solution is manifestly inapplicable to the case of large industry. But though the workers may not be able out of their own resources to find the capital, may they not be able to borrow it in the money market at a fixed interest upon the personal security of their skill, organisation, and contracts? This is in effect what the Building Guild is doing. Its success assumes certain favourable conditions. The first of these is the willing co-operation of the brain workers with the manual workers in the trade. Here the building trade is exceptionally well fitted for the experiment, consisting very largely of small local businesses in which the functions of employer and of craftsman are not sharply differentiated, most employers having come from the ranks of craftsmen and not infrequently combining the two functions. A building group which has taken a contract to put up some houses should be in at least as favourable a position to get the necessary advances to buy materials and pay a few weeks' wages as the small builder who may be one of them, and who has always been in the habit of finding the capital he needs in this way. If an admittedly competent body of brain and hand workers, possessing the necessary tools, can show to financiers that they can make a profit upon their contracts, or upon the sale of the goods they can turn out, they should be able to get the necessary money to finance the operations. Greater difficulty arises where expensive plant and premises are needed, and where the necessary borrowing is larger in amount, for longer periods, and locked up in fixed capital. It ought not, however, to be impossible for the workers to take over a limited number of mines or mills or other businesses in any not too speculative industry through the joint finance of the trade unions and the co-operative movement. For though the savings of the working classes are wholly inadequate to furnish the bulk of the fixed capital involved in their employment, it would easily suffice for certain considerable experiments in this new Industrial Order. This procedure would be a complete overthrow of the domination of capital, establishing in a most practical manner " the dictatorship of the proletariat " within certain areas of industry. Instead of capital hiring labour at a fixed market rate, employing it to work up the materials it owns upon premises it owns or hires, and marketing the product at a price which yields a gain, labour would hire the capital, both fixed and circulating, would be its own employer, market its own goods, and keep for itself the gains. This would be in some sense the most radical of all the new social-economic reforms, ousting the owners of capital from the government of industry and putting labour in their place. The control of the business would be in the hands of the active producers instead of the functionless shareholders. In this way, it is contended, we should elicit the most active energies of brain and hand for the efficiency and progress of the industry.

Treating it, however, as a presently practicable proposal, it would be foolish to pretend that any considerable sections of great industry, or of new and more speculative industry, will pass into this form. The amount of free capital willing to finance at a low fixed return these experimental operations without the usual material guarantees which debenture holders claim must be limited. The willingness of the managerial and technical staffs to quit the employment of capitalism and throw in their lot with their manual employees is as doubtful as is the willingness of the latter to throw aside their suspicions of men whom they have always regarded as belonging to the capitalist side. Probably the social cleavage of classes will present the gravest obstacle of all against an effective co-operation of brain with hand workers in most industries. The " intellectual proletariat " may, indeed, eventually be so reduced in means, education, and " social status," as to recognise a close affinity of interests with organised manual labour, but the approaches of the two in the engineering and a few other trades are yet too shy to promise early and effective solidarity.

We may now conveniently summarise the general types of structural changes by which our industries are striving to adapt themselves to the new situation.

1. Social ownership, in the shape of nationalisation or municipalisation of certain fundamental and essential industries and services, such as mines and railroads, perhaps banking and insurance, with a management as far as possible decentralised and representative of all the activities and interests involved.

2. Guild ownership and management in certain trades where machine production is not the dominant factor, and where effective co-operation between brain workers and hand workers is feasible.

3. Capitalism qualified by a large participation of labour in the management through profit-sharing and co-partnership.

4. Capitalism limited by Wage Boards or other arrangements for securing standard conditions of wages, hours, etc., and adequate provision against unemployment for regular employees.

These are not to be taken as sharply defined classes. Each admits of many modifications and varieties of structure, determined by such conditions as the following : (a) The size of a fully efficient business, especially in regard to capital equipment. (*b*) The amount of competition remaining among the businesses comprising an industry. (*c*) The extent to which mechanical methods of production with routine repetition-work prevail. (*d*) The diversities of technical skill and the sharpness of the cleavage between skilled and unskilled labour in the trade, or between men's and women's work. (*e*) The degree to which an industry is exposed to seasonal, fashion, or cyclical fluctuations of trade. These are but a few of the many considerations which are moulding the shapes of businesses to-day.

Our purpose here, however, is not to express any general judgment upon their character, but to consider the issue of incentives to efficient working among the body of the employees. All aim in different degrees and by different methods to obviate what we held to be the crippling disabilities of the old system, by giving to all classes of labour some stake in the prosperity of the business and some " voice " in its management. The worker is to have a vested interest in the business and in its operation. The capitalist employer is no longer to assert his full right to run his own business in his own way, to buy his labour in a freely competitive market, to use his superior economic power in dictating the terms of employment, and to keep for himself the whole of the profits he can earn. Labour is to have what amounts to an effective participation in the property, proceeds, and control of the business.

How will these various reforms work in the direction of greater productivity? Will they remove the motives which lead labour to restrict output? Will they stimulate an increased energy and a new sense of responsibility? In fine, will the men work better for themselves, their fellows, and the community, than they have lately worked for their masters?

To these really vital questions I can supply no confident reply. I can only point to the probable action of new incentives, not able to measure their strength or width of appeal. Take first what may, without prejudice, be called the most idealist interpretation of a change which eliminates as far as possible " profiteering " as the object of industry and substitutes social service. How far will the fact that the work done no longer contributes to make profits for the capitalist but renders service to the community alter the attitude of mind of the ordinary worker towards his work, making him more willing to do his share? If it be true that some considerable slacking is due to a widespread constant desire to go slow in order to keep down profits, it may seem reasonable that the withdrawal of the profits-motive would liberate this withheld efficiency? But is the mentality of most workers such as will respond effectively to a change to public ownership, under which work for the community presents itself as work for the State? These abstract terms, state, public, community, must carry very little of pleasant emotion to recommend them to a miner or a railway porter, so as to stimulate him to raise his customary output of energy. If he has got the habit of going slow under a company control, is he likely to improve

H

his stroke because the " end " to which his work remotely contributes is no longer profit but public service? Can it be expected that this change of " ends " will penetrate with any emotional significance through the elaborate detailed processes of a complicated industry? Will a hewer ply his pick more quickly or more carefully, will the overlookers and mine managers be keener in planning the exploitation of seams or more careful in arranging for moving the coal, because these officials and miners have become public servants? Will shunters on the railway and platelayers work more energetically, will engine-drivers keep better time, will the loading of freight cars be done quicker and better, because of the consciousness of the new status and end?

It seems possible that so far as ca' canny is a consciously anti-capitalist policy, nationalisation might call it off. But using the term to describe the habit of working at low pressure, it seems exceedingly unlikely that this motive can be dominant in the complex of motives which admittedly prompt labour to resist a driving policy, unlikely that there would emerge any appreciable difference in efficiency. Social service, or the well-being of the community at large, is not likely to have any considerable effect as a motive in the mind of men who continue to do the same work under the same technical conditions and even the same personal control as before. Even in the technical and commercial staff, somewhat more sensible of the meaning of the change, it seems unlikely that there would emerge an appreciable increase in the sense of responsibility or an enhanced desire to work harder or better.

It might be urged that, since the desire to spread employment by working slow is a factor in ca' canny, the greater security of employment under a public service would sap the motive to inefficiency. And this is true, unless it is offset by the removal of the fear of being " fired " for inefficiency, which is the other side of security of employment.

But there is another economic claim for public service which it is convenient to notice here. Remove the profit-making motive, with the insecurity of wages and employment and the speeding up and the bad workmanship which flow therefrom, and put all the brain and manual workers on a truly functional basis as members of a skilled and useful profession. You will, it is urged, evoke those interests of craftsmanship, that desire to do good work, which are withheld and wasted under the present system. But, though I hold it likely that the general escape from the pressure of industry, and particularly machine-industry, on life, should have as its most beneficent effect the liberation of the human instincts of workmanship, I cannot regard this as a fruit directly attainable from nationalisation to any considerable extent. For routine, standardisation, large scale production for the ordinary needs of ordinary people, will continue to be the characteristic of the public services, and the economy of their performance prescribes minute specialisation and subdivision of labour which, though calling for high qualities of efficiency, do not permit that liberty of personal expression which is the essence of true craftsmanship. In other words, I do not deem it likely that the elimination or modification of profiteering in the New Order will make work appreciably more interesting or attractive in the industries brought under the new conditions. The compensations have, I think, to be looked for outside the routine services, in the enlargement of leisure and other opportunities that should accrue from the greater ease and security of the New Order.

But, it may be said, if no increased productivity is to be got from the incentive of social service or from the instinct of workmanship, upon what can we rely as incentives adequate to maintain industrial efficiency and progress? The answer, I hold, must be " on the merits of representative government." Autocracy has failed in industry, as it has failed in politics. The democratic institutions which have displaced it in the latter sphere have plenty of faults. But nobody seriously regards it as practicable to return to the Autocratic State. Absolute government did work in industry, it may continue to work in some countries, and in some industries here. But it has broken down in the larger departments of great capitalism, and must be replaced by methods better adjusted to the psychology of the new situation. This cannot be done by substituting a directly social interest and gain for an individual interest and gain, but by giving new expression and validity to the latter. As a free citizen, who has a voice in the city government and knows that he stands to gain by helping to make it good, is more socially useful than a bondsman or an inert taxpayer, so with the member of a trade. He tends to work better and to see that others work better, and so to evolve a public opinion in favour of good work, if there is thrown on him a direct right and responsibility to control the *near* conditions of good work. I emphasise the word " *near* " because it brings out the essential condition of success. Experience of political democracy shows that its real, perhaps only success, is in small areas of government. Democracy and a great empire are incompatible. The conditions of industrial democracy drive home the same truth most forcibly.

No object would be served by discussing here the particular forms of representation suited to industries in their several sizes and structures. The workshop is the natural unit of self-government where available, the area in which the individual workers are thrown into close and constant association for purposes related to their common conditions of employment and those outside conditions of neighbourhood and society dependent on the former. Most men's minds do not habitually travel very far. Representative government, therefore, depends on organising small groups of workers in such close and constant contact that they know what one another is doing and more or less what one another is thinking and feeling. This common knowledge is the basis of all sound representation. What the group wants is someone competent to look after the interests its members have in common. Though a genuine and wider *esprit de corps* may be evolved, by which the members of these little groups will subordinate their narrower views and interests to the wider ones of a whole trade or a labour movement, the real grip of self-government lies in the close contacts of the workshop group. The special craft-spirit may overlap and sometimes conflict with this workshop spirit, uniting members of different businesses, or even industries, by tighter bonds of interest than are presented by common employment in a workshop or a mine. But the recent continuous advance of industrial unionism seem to testify to the truth that the personal close contacts of individuals in their daily work give the chief force which ought to be organisable for representative government in industry. We have seen that the actual movements of the time are along this line, shop committees, trades boards, Whitley Councils, and the like. There can be no single type or pattern for these units of industrial self-government or for their federations in wider areas. Variations must correspond to the different economic structures of each trade or plant. But certain general principles will be observed. All "functional" services must be represented at each stage and the representation should be proportional. But proportional to what? To mere numbers? Surely not. For in that case the Government would in most instances be in the hands of a numerical majority of unskilled or low-skilled workers. Clearly representation should be proportional to the importance of the function, not to the mere number of those exercising it. But where each function, i.e., that of managerial and technical skill, that of manual labour and of the supply of capital, is essential to the conduct of the industry, they may be presumed to have an equal importance for purpose of representation. It may, however, very well be true of certain types of business that the difference of interests between skilled and unskilled manual labour, or even between the commercial and the technical staffs, is such as to make separate representation desirable.

Since the direct object of such a representative government would be to secure prosperity for all the members of the business or the industry, it is evident that its success will depend on mobilising group opinion in favour of efficiency and productivity by appeals to group interest. Government is always a means, never an end. The test of a good industrial government will be whether each constituent unit gets from it a satisfactory gain. The ultimate unit is the individual worker, but representative government looks to group opinion and interest for its potency. What the worker will continue to be after, and what underlies all the demands for " status " and representative government, is pay, security of livelihood, hours and other conditions, all dependent on and derived from the prosperous and efficient working of the business. These new securities for labour can only be got by means of this representation, but they can only be made economically feasible on condition that they work towards efficiency and productivity. And these pressures and incentives towards productivity will be group forces acting in and through individual minds.

THE NEW INDUSTRIAL ORDER

Community of business interests is not inaptly conveyed by the term profit-sharing, provided no close definition of profit be pressed, and reflections upon the past history of profit-sharing are exceedingly instructive in its bearing upon our problem. In most instances the experiment of offering the workers in a big business a share of any extra profits beyond those required to pay a fixed dividend proved a failure, and the reasons for the failure are not obscure. To tell a man that, if he and ten thousand of his fellows work harder or better, they will each get a minute fraction of the product of this harder or better work a year hence, provided the increased product is not previously absorbed in paying current wages and profits, is not " good enough," i.e., does not provide an effective and continuous incentive. But supposing you were to tell the same man that, if he and his four mates working together in the same shop and on the same job put through more work they would get for certain a considerable bonus every month, or every three months, you would bring to bear a real incentive to efficiency. Not only would he see and feel that he was getting a direct personal gain for his extra exertion, but he would see and feel that the size of that gain depended on his mates keeping pace with his increased energy. He would also be aware that each of his mates had his eye on him to see that he did his share. In other words, this small group gain becomes an effective economic incentive, provided also it is near and certain.

Where profit-sharing appears to have succeeded on a large group basis, as in certain gas undertakings, there is a special explanation. In all such cases there has been either a legalised monopoly or some such control of markets as has given the business in question a power to earn profits considerably above the ordinary competitive level. In other words, the workers have been promised and obtained a share of a surplus gain not due merely to their own efficiency or energy, but largely to some limited power to overcharge consumers. The enhanced value of the share thus secured to them, together with the greater certainty of getting it, may have evoked some increased energy from large bodies of workers, in spite of the fact that each only get a very small fraction of the advantage of his own increased exertion. Competitive industry, however, could furnish no such supplement. Any success of profit-sharing in a competitive business would depend entirely on the efficacy of the incentive in the individual worker. In that efficacy there will be four factors, the size of the gain, its certainty, its nearness in time, and the strength of the group pressure on the individual will.

I do not wish to undervalue the contribution towards improved efficiency of brain and manual labour which may come from a " new social atmosphere," the sense of dignity and responsibility of workers who are no longer engaged in selling their labour-power in detachable pieces to be put into goods and marketed for the benefit of capitalist employers, but who are conscious of working for themselves, their comrades, and the public in an industry which in some true sense belongs to them and in the government of which they have a powerful voice. This new status, even if it cannot be relied upon to yield a strong new stimulus to improved discipline and increased efficiency, should at least get rid of the positive resentment against masterhood and profiteering which may be a considerable factor in restricting output. Though it may not stop strikes, it should make them far less frequent, by reason of the improved community of interests and the representative character of the government.

But the great immediate gains to productivity may be expected to come less from this diffused sense of common interest than from the closer personal and group appeals which may arise from schemes of bonuses, profiteering, co-partnership, when these schemes are no longer devised, organised, and administered automatically by the management, with some carefully restricted participation by the workers, but are a part of the ordinary machinery of administration in a self-governing business. Group self-discipline within the workshop or other industrial unit may become the most potent incentive to increased productivity where it is definitely and securely associated with tangible gains to each member of the groups. The yield of such incentives must, of course, vary largely with the technical conditions of the particular work, and will usually be least where machine-production is most highly developed, greatest where essentially dull or repellent work has been left to human muscles or brains under conditions of lax supervision. Though no close estimates of slack in the working of any industry are available, war experience everywhere revealed a quite astonishing amount of it, by showing the large results of patriotic and other special stimuli in accelerating the pace and energy of the individual workers and in promoting effective co-operation. These results were produced, moreover, in spite of great dislocations and rapid improvisations and of the existence of governmental interferences often exceedingly unwise and wasteful. Making due allowance for these offsets, it does not seem unreasonable to believe that (with proper deductions for the excessive pressure of war-work) the pre-war slack, represented by " ca' canny," days off, strikes and lockouts, short time and trade depressions, wasteful competition in distribution, amounted to one third, if not one half of the available productive power of the nation. How much of this slack is due to the ca' canny and other labour motives, how much to incompetent management or a restrictive policy of capital, may be argued endlessly in each instance. But nobody seriously disputes the fact that bricklayers could increase their toll of bricks by, say 50%, without injurious over-exertion, if they felt it to be worth while, and that the same holds of very large bodies of other time workers in the building, transport, engineering and distributive trades, while the normal pace of piece-work in most occupations where this method of payment prevails, is by habit or agreement kept down towards the level of the slower or less efficient workers in the trade. So far as this is true it marks a signal failure of incentives in the present capitalist system. The new Industrial Order might reasonably expect that its abolition or restriction of profiteering, on the one hand, and its new status for labour in a self-governing business or industry, on the other, would be able to make considerable drafts upon these hitherto withheld sources of productivity.

If, however, this result is to be obtained, the forms of industrial self-government must be adapted to the special technique and organisation of each industrial process. For, in order to stimulate the will to efficiency among the workers, the psychology of group incentives must be studied in relation to the technique of each sort of work. A given quantity of gain attainable in a given time will operate very differently among a group of skilled compositors and a similar-sized group of spade labourers, and differently according as the group is directly co-operating towards a single action, as in the rowing of a fishing boat, co-operating towards a single but divisible process as in the unloading of a cargo, or, finally co-operating by sharp division of labour in which each man's job dovetails into that of his neighbour. But while the diffused goodwill of the members of a group or gang is an important element in the efficient running of a business, there is another of equally critical importance, viz., the automatic response to detailed orders. Unless the intro-duction of the self-governing principle into the workshop and industry is consistent with this unquestioning response, the requisite amount of work will not get done : processes will not run smoothly. A good deal of loss of time and energy is at present due to resentment of the domineering ways of foremen and others in autocratic authority. But in a self-governing workshop some one must be invested with an authority to give orders which workers, or comrades, must obey. Complete confidence in the general acceptance of orders from the persons who are chosen to be overseers or managers, either directly by the workers whom they oversee, or indirectly by their representatives, is an essential condition of workshop efficiency. The common charge against experiments in self-government is that the men will not obey these orders of their elected chiefs, and will not invest them with the requisite powers of discipline. It is not, however, necessary to affirm that workshop self-government will yield perfect discipline, but only that it will yield better discipline than is now and henceforward attainable upon the alternative plan, which, effective in a more submissive state of the working class mind, is no longer so. The willingness to take orders will be a chief test of the new consciousness of industrial democracy. Obedience to the laws which we have helped to make depends upon a realising sense that the laws are of our own making. It is often confidently asserted that workers will have less respect for their own officials than for those set over them by employers, and that these officials, aware that they cannot exercise discipline, will connive at laxity. Here is the supreme problem of morals and intelligence. It is the crux of democracy in whatever field of conduct. Many consider that political democracy has failed, or is failing, precisely because of the inability or unwillingness of the individual citizen to realise that it is to his interest to choose good representatives, to trust them when chosen, and to carry out the laws they have passed. Will industrial democracy fare any better in this crucial test? It is a great psychological experiment. It may be admitted that, unless the worker rallies to this call on personal responsibility better than the citizen, the industrial organisation we contemplate will prove unworkable. But there are two grounds of hope. The failure, or grave deficiency of political self-government is largely attributable to two causes, the size of electoral and governmental areas and the vagueness of the ends or gains of political action. Citizens do not care enough about politics because they do not realise adequately that they individually can exercise any power or get any gain. It should be different in such industrial self-government as we here envisage. The electoral and governmental areas must, we recognise, be small, and the gains considerable, material, assured and near. In other words, workers may be expected to choose reliable officials and to do what these tell them, if they can be got to a conscious and continuous realisation of the fruits of this discipline. Here is a wide field of experiment for the economic psychologist, to devise methods of representation applicable to the technical conditions of the various kinds of work, which shall evoke by personal and group incentives of strong continuous interest this genuine self-government.

CHAPTER VI

THE INTERESTS OF CONSUMERS

GUIDED more by convenience than by strict logic I have so far left almost entirely out of consideration that exceedingly important factor in industry, the consumer. Though formally ascribing to him a place in the directorate of industry, I have left that place undefined. Nor does this omission .seem quite unnatural and improper to most who are concerned with the reformed structure and conduct of an industry. The consumer, they would say, does not directly function in the industry, although the industry exists in order to supply his wants and his demand impresses itself upon the conduct of the industry. In fact, so long as the competitive principle actively prevailed, the needs and interests of consumers seemed to require no other safeguard than the intelligent self-regard of the competing businesses. Every improvement in the arts of production eventually must come home to the consumer in reduced prices or better and more abundant goods. In rare instances it might be necessary to furnish legal protection to the innocent consumer against adulterated or otherwise injurious goods, but even here the accepted rule was *caveat emptor*. In general, though the consumer, strictly speaking, stood outside the machinery of industry, his will was able to exercise a dominant control, compelling the organisers and managers of industry to produce goods in such quantities and kinds, and to sell them on such terms as were conducive to the interests of consumers. This, of course, even in competitive industry was not the whole story. The consumers will and his " effective demand " did not function with perfect freedom of initiative. The skill and interest of producers were directed to stimulate and direct consumption by various arts of suggestion. But, so long as competition of producers was free and effective, the consumer got what he wanted upon fairly reasonable terms. Indeed, as we have already noted, the constant tendency towards overproduction in most branches of manufacture and commerce in ordinary times played into his hands. Where there are more willing sellers than buyers, where supply tends to outrun demand, the consumer's external control over industry is fully adequate to protect his interests. But where competition gives way to combination of producers, and in times when shortages of materials, transport, labour, or finance restrict the output or supply, the weakness of the consumer becomes apparent. He then finds his convenience or comfort, perhaps his very life, at the mercy of some business group in control of the shortage, who may find their gain in extorting high prices for a restricted output. The squeeze may be exercised by cornering the supply of some essential commodity, such as wool, copper or oil, or by control of storage or of transport, or by some combine of manufacturers or merchants either along the main road of production or in some subsidiary bypath. The combine may rest on some basis of natural scarcity or superiority of resources, on the monopoly of patents or other technical economies, on tariff protection or other state aids, on strong finance, exceptional skill of organisation, or upon a simple appeal to the obvious interests of competitors to save the risks and waste of cut-throat competition. Varying greatly in strength and in degree of control, according to the intrinsic importance of the goods or services in question, the existence of accessible and effective substitutes, the completeness of the combination and the existence of potential competition, these combinations for control of selling prices are everywhere spreading throughout the fields of manufacture, transport, commerce and finance. Everywhere they imperil the interests of the consumer. For engaged primarily and avowedly in maintaining prices at a " reasonably profitable " level, they are able to raise them to a point determined by the consumers' needs expressed in elasticity of demand. That is to say they aim at taking " all the trade will bear."

A trust, cartel, or other combine does not necessarily raise prices. It may find it more profitable simply to absorb the savings that come from stopping the costs of competition and from improved methods of production and organisation, economies which might otherwise have gone to reduce prices. But generally it will also pay to raise prices, at any rate at certain times and over certain areas of market. The normal effect of such combination is to restrict output, and to sell

I

the smaller supply at a higher price, or at any rate to cancel that tendency towards full supply, wherein lay the safety of the consumer under the system of free competition.

The general stimulation of organisation and combination given by war requirements and controls, the natural and artificial shortages due to post-war conditions and policies, the financial weakness of small businesses during the violent fluctuations of prices and exchange which mark the post-war period, have greatly accelerated the combinatory movement in this and other countries. But when I affirm that the consumer is now in need of a protection which he did not need before, I must remind readers that the term consumer is by no means confined to the ultimate purchasers of commodities, but comprises in different relations every class of producer who requires to purchase from other trades his materials, tools, fuel, and other goods. For though the ultimate incidence of the surplus profits which combines seek to secure is piled on to the prices which the final consumer pays, none the less are the interests of the productive consumer deeply involved in the operations of combines controlling articles they need for their businesses. It is, of course, of vital importance to all users of industrial power that coal, oil, electricity shall not be vested in private combines. For a rise in the cost of power must tend to curtail their output and raise their prices while lowering their aggregate profits, if they are members of a competitive industry. The monopolistic control of a number of materials in the building trade is not only injurious to the general population, who cannot get housing at any reasonable price, but to builders and contractors whose market is thus reduced, and to all employers and workers in other trades ancillary to building who enjoy no such pull themselves.

But the interests of consumers in the administration of industry is by no means confined to cases of trusts or combinations which monopolise markets and control prices. Wherever capital and labour in a trade are organised, severally or in concert, for the regulation, by agreement, of wages and other conditions of employment, the use of machinery and other technical methods of production, buying and selling processes, tariff and other trade relations, the vital interests of consumers are clearly involved, and do not always square with those of the producers. Now, as we know, machinery for adjusting the interests of the capital and labour in those industries where some measure of competition survives is everywhere in process of erection, whether in the form of Boards of Conciliation, Trade Boards, Whitley Councils, or otherwise. The trade regulations which may emerge from such bodies, looking solely to the immediate interests of employers and employed, may, especially in trades not exposed to foreign competition, involve high expenses which, even without express price-agreements, will be loaded on to the consumer. The adoption of improved machinery, or other changes requiring large capital expenditure, may be delayed out of sheer conservatism or to avert labour troubles. Apart from the positive injuries which such productive policies may inflict on consumers, these trade organisations will often be irresponsive to the changing needs and tastes of the consuming public.

If consumers are to exercise that influence upon the machinery of industry to which they are entitled, they must have some representation in the government of the trades which exist to supply their wants. Nor can it suffice to leave the protection of their interests to the Board of Trade or any other body of State officials. For, though the State may legitimately claim to exercise some general control over industrial action in matters of public order or hygiene, it cannot be regarded as a sufficient guardian of the consumer. For the consuming public is highly differentiated in its interests and its attitude towards the different industries that serve it. This has been recently recognised in such proposals as were made in the majority Report of the Coal Commission in this country and in the Plumb Plan for the government of American railroads. The Sankey Commission gave a definite representation to the different bodies of large productive consumers in the several areas of mining administration. In the new plan by which our railways are forced into amalgamations a grave defect is the absence of any direct provision for the representation of the collieries and other big shippers upon the controlling bodies. For it cannot be admitted that the representation of their interests can be adequately rendered by the Committee of the Board of Trade. Still less is it the case that the interests of the private individual consumers of such commodities as coal or railway services can be entrusted solely to State officials, or to the chance of certain large consumers sitting on the directorate of a mining or railway company.

However difficult it may be to secure representation of private consumers, the attempt should be made. Over large areas of working class population the vigorous Co-operative Movement affords an obviously suitable instrument for such representation. But though the wholesale and retail traders associations, Chambers of Commerce, etc., might perform a highly serviceable function in protecting the interests of distributors, it would be foolish to pretend that the final consumers' interests would be safe in their hands. For apart from the strong control which manufacturing combines often exercise over the distribution of the goods they produce, the squeezing of the final consumer by organised traders is one of the most dangerous features of the present business world. As the displacement of competition by combination everywhere proceeds, and the problem of high prices and profiteering under private enterprise presses ever more onerously on the consuming public, the demand for national ownership and democratic control should be fortified by the formation of consumers associations in order to furnish an essential factor of industrial self-government.

Now combinations of consumers, known as the Co-operative Societies, already play a considerable part in the control of industry. Their members number nearly four millions out of the ten million families, their one thousand five hundred stores supply annually some two hundred million pounds worth of household goods, their wholesale trade amounts to a hundred million pounds : they possess their own factories, farms, shops, insurance and banking, all run without profit upon capital for the benefit of the consumer. The groups of local consumers subscribe the share capital required to stock and run the store, and elect the managing committee that appoints the store-staff and directs the business. These local autonomous Co-operative Societies are represented, through persons chosen by their committees, upon the English and Scottish Wholesale Societies, which between them do a business of over a hundred million pounds per annum, and a banking turnover of more than five hundred millions sterling.

Thus it appears that some five or six per cent of the business of the nation is already under consumers' control, and enthusiastic co-operators set no limits to its advance. Closer inquiry into its history and present condition, however, does not encourage the expectation that it will displace private capitalism in the largest enterprises, where a great share capital is required and high risks are run, or where, as in most branches of agriculture and in the production of finer and more individual commodities, high qualities of skill and adaptation enter. The provision, however, of certain standard household goods, may pass more and more into this type of business, and the Co-operative Movement may here perform an important function as a check upon the control of such commodities by capitalist combinations.

THE INTERESTS OF CONSUMERS

But when we regard the Co-operative Movement as an experiment in industrial democracy it
is impossible to ignore certain defects derived from
the assumption that the consumers' interests are
paramount and the consumers' control is absolute.
Though in the local societies the quarterly members'
meetings provide a more effective and continuous
contact between management and consumers than
the ordinary joint-stock company between management and shareholders, it is difficult where the
membership is large for any appreciable number
of them to take any intelligent part in the control.
And, when we pass from the local society to the
wider business operations of the Wholesale
Societies, the electoral machinery out of which the
committee is evolved works with some difficulty.
The great mass of co-operators can have no real
knowledge even of the men who govern the Wholesale in their name. " If," write Mr and Mrs
Webb,[1] " we ask how far this great democratic
organisation exhibits the characteristics of the
ideal democracy of popular aspiration, it is
difficult to ignore the allegation that it has some
of the weaknesses of an honest but somewhat im-
pervious bureaucracy—secretiveness, a dislike of
publicity, an impatience of criticism, and, it is
commonly alleged, a certain amount of favouritism
in appointments and promotions. All this is the
more dangerous in that the whole administration
is wrapped in obscurity, without the publication
of salary lists, details of costing, or anything

[1] A Constitution for the Socialist Commonwealth of
Great Britain, p. 258.

beyond a bare minimum of comparative statistics enabling the members to watch for themselves the relative expense or efficiency of the various departments." To this difficulty in making consumers' democracy real and effective is added the danger lest in the absence of direct representation the interest of co-operative employees should be unduly sacrificed to dividends. In other words, in a movement where comparatively few of the co-operators are employed in co-operative undertakings, producer may be sacrificed to consumer. Only by linking up more closely the trade union with the co-operative movement can this defect find its natural remedy.

Outside the co-operative movement a few not very effective attempts have been made at organisation of consumers' interests in the supply of special goods or services. Railway users and coal consumers have shown some capacity of local organisation for the protection of their interests. But such functional representation can only be made effective if it is incorporated in the actual control and administration of the industry.

In asserting this right to a voice in the government of industry for the consumer one need not, however, envisage the latter as taking a full and equal share in the direction or management of an industry with the representatives of capital and labour engaged therein. Consumers' representatives would not claim a direct share in business administration. They would rather hold a watching brief over the conduct of the business, only intervening where the interests of their clients were clearly involved. Those cases would be chiefly of two kinds, where wasteful, obsolete, or expensive methods of technique or administration were practised for the convenience or advantage of one or other of the factors of production, and where combined action of producing firms was oppressive to consumers in price or qualities of goods or services. What the consumer needs for his protection is more of the nature of a veto than of a positive direction. Or perhaps we should rather say that his representation is required to quicken and enforce the imperfect veto which he already exercises through his demand for commodities. The natural normal check upon raising of prices and other abuses of producers' power is a withholding or reduction of demand. Where competition of producers remains effective, this check is fairly adequate. But where combination or concerted action of producers supervenes, it is not adequate, and requires to be reinforced by some more direct control.

The importance of securing the safety of the consumer and the progressive standard of consumption is seen to have a special urgency, not merely from the fact that consumption is the end or object of production, but because what we term the natural control of consumption over production has got out of gear. As we have already shown, there has been exhibited in modern capitalism a serious tendency for the rate of production to outstrip the rate of consumption, so that the productive machinery is periodically pulled up nearly to a standstill, because the goods which it is capable of turning out cannot get sold and consumed fast enough. That this is not due to mere miscalculation or misapplication of productive resources is proved by its general and simultaneous occurrence in most industries and most countries. It is a failure of consumption to keep pace with production, due primarily to the failure of the terms at which goods are offered in the market to stimulate and evoke an effective demand from consumers. This phenomenon may be explained, either in terms of the excessive price at which goods are offered, or of the defective incomes applicable to their purpose. These two explanations are evidently the convex and the concave of the same fact. That maldistribution of income which puts too much of it in the possession of idle possessors or over-remunerated organisers of finance and industrial power, too little in the possession of the rank and file of the working populations, causes too large a proportion to be expended on capital goods and on luxuries, too little in the regular demand and consumption of the ever-growing quantities of standard commodities which capitalistic industry is capable of turning out.

This is where a juster and better distribution would react upon the volume and character of productive industry. Remove the surplus unearned income which at present goes as economic rents, excessive interest, profits or other emoluments of strongly organised or protected business men, and apply it, either by taxation to productive public services, or by the organised pressure of labour and state policy to increased wages, two important reactions upon production and employment will ensue. The higher regular standard both of public and of private demand for commodities will afford full and regular employment to the capital and labour in all the standard industries. Secondly, a constantly increasing differentiation will take place in the higher levels of the consumption of the workers. Instead of confining their effective demand to what may be termed routine material requisites, such as can only be produced by mechanical and uninteresting labour, a growing proportion of spending power will be devoted to demand for individual forms of satisfaction which call for higher qualities of skill in their production. Progress in civilisation may be measured by and largely consists in this broad diffusion of a standard of life containing larger elements of consumption which express the individual needs, tastes, and interests of consumers. The dominion of machine-production can thus be checked and balanced by an increase of those finer applications of productive energy required for the higher qualities of material wealth and for those immaterial goods and personal services the demand for which at present is confined to the capricious and disordered tastes and enjoyments of the privileged few. A just and more equal distribution of income is, therefore, a prime condition both of a fuller and more regular volume of employment and of that reduction in the monotonous routine of labour which is its heaviest human cost. Such an economic policy yields new incentives and a truer meaning to that higher productivity of which at present we so idly prate.

CHAPTER VII

THE GOVERNMENT OF INDUSTRY

OUR plan has been to consider one by one the several activities which go to make up modern industry and to ascertain whether the incentives needed to evoke and sustain their activities are likely to be obtainable in a new Industrial Order where the chief fundamental industries have passed from private profitable enterprise into social services, publicly owned and administered by bodies representative of all the producing and consuming factors, and where most other industries, engaged in supplying primary needs by routine or standardised methods, are brought under some representative control as regards conditions of labour, prices and security of supply. While recognising that industries will differ widely in the relative importance assigned to the several activities of the inventor and organiser, the technical expert, the financier, the providers of share and debenture capital, the directorate and the managerial staff, the skilled and unskilled labour employed, we found that the doubts and difficulties of those who question the feasibility of the New Order everywhere turn upon certain crucial matters of incentive.

THE GOVERNMENT OF INDUSTRY

Will a sufficient amount of saving take place when some of the most profitable fields of investment are removed from private enterprise and when a more equal distribution of net incomes reduces those great funds of wealth which automatically accumulate as capital after their possessors have spent all they desire to spend? Will great inventive and organising talent, foresight, initiative, audacity and enterprise, be available for the promotion of industrial progress? Will expert knowledge of business and technology, with the qualities of application, responsibility, tact, and judgment, which go so far towards competent management, be forthcoming under national ownership and representative control? Finally, will the employees under the new Industrial Order give out a sufficient quantity of productive energy and care, and will they submit to efficient workshop discipline?

In endeavouring to answer these questions I have given chief prominence to the following considerations. First, that the higher qualities of inventiveness and enterprise are relatively less important in those industries which are ripe for public ownership and representative government than in those which, being in a more flexible and experimental stage, remain proper subjects for private enterprise. Secondly, that there is reason to believe that great powers of business administration and of resourcefulness are often found in men whose public spirit and high regard for public reputation will lead them to prefer the career of a distinguished official to that of a successful moneymaker. Thirdly, that the efficiency and discipline of employees, considerably impaired under the present capitalist system, may be restored by removing certain of the causes which impair it, notably that fear of unemployment which is the chief feeder of " ca' canny," and may even be rendered more effective by reasonable stimuli of gain applied to small working groups. Finally, that the new combinative character of many modern industries requires the consumer, or the market, to be recognised as a determinant factor of industry, by means of representation in any body set up for the government of industry.

The method adopted in these chapters is, however, obviously defective as a contribution to the psychology of industrial reform in one essential. It has been decided to economise motives, regarded exclusively from the standpoint of separate businesses and industries. But some of our gravest modern problems are concerned with the discovery of principles and practices for the ordering of industry as a whole, both as regards the inter-relations of the several industries and the place which industry shall occupy in the State. Though a full discussion of these problems, so profitably raised by such writers as Mr R. H. Tawney, Mr G. D. H. Cole and others, is here impossible, I feel compelled to a brief statement of the bearing of the present treatment of economic incentives upon these wider aspects of industrial and social unity. While in close sympathy with the ethical spirit which marks Mr Tawney's powerful indictment of the acquisitive principle in industry, and his desire to see the several industries set upon a basis of social function, I cannot regard such a radical reconstruction as immediate and generally attainable. Personal selfishness can no more be eliminated from the performance of any social function, than physical force from the practices of government. In proportion as the modes of industry can be made skilful, intelligible, interesting, and light, the acquisitive motive may be displaced from its dominance by other motives, the satisfaction of the instinct of workmanship, the glory of achievement, public esteem, some genuine sense of social service. All skilful work carries with it a measure of this appeal, and a skilled craftsman, reasonably certain of his livelihood, escapes the worst poison of acquisitiveness. But this is not to say that his pay is no incentive. Still less can it be maintained that such a craftsman, or even artist, will not remain acquisitive in other ways. Pride of personal achievement, the satisfaction in the exercise of personal skill and the love of popular applause, remain expressions of the acquisitive spirit. Self-importance or the pride of power, which is a staple of these emotions, are no more elevating morally than the desire of gain. Moreover, as we have seen, most of those activities which are most socially serviceable in their ends are least susceptible to the joys and interests of skilled personal achievement. Though an intelligent education may evoke some sense of dignity and social utility in the performance of these intrinsically dull and laborious " functions," they can hardly be expected to displace the direct interest of pay in a miner or a railway man. It is impossible to expect to get the acquisitive spirit out of industry. It will always continue to be an important incentive, though to some extent it may be modified. Security of tenure and of the standard of living will modify it. Interest or dignity of employment may drive it below the level of clear consciousness, as in the performance of most skilled professional work. But it would be undesirable to pretend that the cruder egoism of personal gain can be expelled from any employment, so that the sense of the performance of a social function may take its place. It would be far better to recognise " acquisitiveness " as a motive of industry which can be made available for socially useful work, and to direct it economically to this end.

Now any analysis of the actual distribution of wealth shows that the motive of acquisitiveness is applied most wastefully. Economic rents, surplus profits, and other excessive payments, not only fail as incentives to evoke productive energy, but operate in two ways to reduce its output. For this unearned surplus, enabling its recipients to live without work, is an inducement to idleness. On the other hand, by reducing the total fund of income available otherwise for stimulating the productivity of brain or hand labour in industry, it keeps that output lower than it would have been.

Though distribution according to needs is the ethical ideal, and should everywhere be recognised in the provision of a full subsistence for all members of society as the first claim upon the annual product of industry, this principle must be qualified for action by a due recognition of the permanent character of the acquisitive instinct. This instinct should be harnessed to the car of industrial progress, and not treated as a baseness to be stamped out of a more elevated social system. Everything which education and environment can do to encourage the sense of social service and to moderate the lust of personal gain, should be done. But that lust will not disappear, and it is capable of being made to contribute results that are socially valuable in themselves. Our analysis goes further than this in repudiating the sharp antithesis of an acquisitive and functional society. It insists that for practical present purposes, it is necessary to leave a large industrial field open to the " predatory instincts," safeguarding society in other ways against the anti-social consequences which may ensue, and securing for society as large a share of the predatory gain as can be annexed without undue interference with the profit-making motive.

The industrial system thus envisaged consists, partly of nationalised industries, operated by representative government, partly of private industries working either by automatic competition or by some scheme of profit-sharing or co-operation, with provisions for safeguarding the primary interests of workers and consumers. Though this mixed system does not bring up in its sharpest shape the question of the relations between the several industries, it is impossible to ignore this question. Assuming that it were possible to maintain a complex of incentives adequate for harmony and efficiency of working in and among the business units of the great nationalised industries, how are these industries themselves to be wrought into harmony as a national system? Modify as you may, or even depose, the acquisitive instinct as the ruling incentive in the several businesses comprising a national industry, there will remain the risk of the instinct reasserting itself in the industry as an aggregate. All industries are not equally vital or fundamental. What principle is to regulate the dealings of these unequal industries with one another, so as to prevent the more vital and fundamental from taking advantage of the inherent strength of their position to secure an undue share of the social product? The issue is a very real one. Although we may readily condemn a proposal directly and openly to tax other industries for the maintenance of employment and wages in the mines, we cannot so easily dispose of the " national " endeavour of miners, railwaymen or other key-groups, to insist on rates of pay or hours of labour or other expensive conditions which measure not their needs, or the intrinsic value of their services, but their relative strength as bargainers. This difficulty is most prone to arise in times like the present, when rapid and large fluctuations of prices and of trade conditions justify and, indeed, compel frequent adjustments of wage-rates. Nationalised, or otherwise withdrawn from anything that could be called free competition, how is it possible for owners or workers to know what is a reasonable rate of profits or of wages? In default of any standard, what more natural than that a strongly-placed trade should take as much as it can get? So agriculture seeks everywhere to bleed the town industrialists, while town industries retort by the pressure of cartels and other combines, shipping seizes every opportunity to squeeze the traffic by extortionate freights, bankers restrict the supply of credit and raise its prices, and every trade which is temporarily or locally in a place of vantage, seeks to make all it can out of it.

In the new Industrial Order we describe it will be of paramount importance to protect society against this broad play of the acquisitive spirit in pulls of the more powerful industries at the expense of the weaker. Otherwise, little may be gained even by the most successful experiments in harmonising capital and labour in the several industries. Social strife, conducted between industry and industry, between agriculture and town work, between workers in extractive industry and workers in the later manufacturing stages, may be as wasteful and as perilous as the struggle between capital and labour which it may displace.

To some reformers a Guild or Functional Congress seems to afford a satisfactory method of reconciling these oppositions of interests. No single trade or group of trades (as for example a Triple Alliance) would be able to get more, or give less, than they deserve, because any attempt to do so would be met and frustrated by the other trades actuated by a policy of common self-defence! But this reliance upon a Balance of Power would be as unsatisfactory in industry as it has proved to be in politics, and for the same reason. It presents no true harmony of interests and no organic policy. We may speak of functional representation in such a Congress or Parliament, but no organic unity is brought into being to which these social functions attach. In other words, there has not emerged an industrial society, whose general welfare directs the special functions. As in politics, the term Balance of Power resolves itself into a policy of Pulls, distribution alike of effort and of product being determined by the relative strength of the parties or groups. This must be so in a Congress or Parliament representative, avowedly, not of any common interest or purpose, but of the particular interests and purposes of the various groups. The mining, or railroad, or electrical or banking representatives, on such a body, desiring chiefly the prosperity and progress of their own industry, will necessarily overvalue its claims. The fact that every industry will be similarly affected will not yield a socially satisfactory resultant. For, as no reasonable or equitable principle, no truly organic law, is of general acceptance, as nobody is there to look after the good of the whole community, there is no alternative to economic force as arbiter. It will not, indeed, pay the mining or any other strong industry to abuse its power beyond a certain limit, lest the injury it works on other industries comes home in deprivation of the goods or services they render. But within those limits, often wide, force may run riot, animosities be inflamed, and wide conflicts of interest ensue.

It may be said that such consumers' representation in the several trades as we have contemplated is an adequate prevision against any real abuse of power. But this is not the case. For guild representation will evoke issues in which the interests of the producers as a body will be opposed to those of the consumers. The issue then arises how a veto of the consumers may be made effective. Take a concrete instance, not necessarily one directly affecting wages, the natural resistance which capital and labour in a manufacturing trade may make to the introduction of new and disturbing processes or machinery. The consumers, the social interest, is served by a rapid adoption of these improvements, which will lower the costs of production and prices, or perhaps produce a better or more various supply. Professional conservatism will always be prone to resist such disturbing innovations. What means will a professional congress possess for making either the interest of other trades which are affected, or the welfare of the consuming public, prevail? Will talk or moral suasion make men adopt and work efficiently machinery they do not like, or accept a standard of pay or other conditions which they find unsatisfactory? The term " general will " may be difficult of definition and of application, but it must in some form stand at the back of all government which deserves the name social. In other words, a new industrial order cannot dispense with the ultimate sovereignty of the State. Society cannot live on separate functions which are not functions of any organism but run " upon their own." There must be some body competent to compare the respective claims of the several industries, and this body must represent the citizen-consumers, for only in their lives and welfare do the claims under consideration find an organic contact.

Mr Cole may endeavour to break up his human beings into a number of separate functions, each capable of representation in a special guild, and may challenge us to find any remainder, or any general quality of humanity, which needs representation.[1] But this is only the old quandary of philosophers, the reconcilement of the one with the many. The unity or general humanity of a person co-exists with his aspects or functions. It not only requires recognition, but it asserts sovereignty. Thus only can we get even a semblance of harmony into what is otherwise a social anarchy. It is not, however, necessary to labour the philosophic aspect of this need of a State or unified social authority, however elected or appointed. For, in our detailed discussion we have discovered certain functions which cannot be performed by any body which does not represent the wholeness of society. I do not refer to those activities of defence or other distinctively non-economic functions which less extreme Guild Socialists would leave to some attenuated State. I mean the specifically economic functions of securing and directing the flow of new industrial power, the fresh funds of capital and labour needed for the maintenance and growth of industry. The all-important processes of evoking

[1] *Cf.* his " Social Theory," p. 108.

and apportioning new brains, labour power, and savings, to the various economic needs, can only be performed by a body in origin and nature independent of these specific economic functions. The general activities of education and of social finance will be the chief instruments of a control which the State, with its ultimately coercive powers for the preservation of social order, will exercise in adjusting the claims of the several industries in their relations to one another and to the consumer-citizen. The intellectual and moral claim of the State to this sovereignty is based upon its representation, in however imperfect a manner, of the common welfare of the nation, as contrasted with the representation of the several, separate, and frequently conflicting interests, of the industries.

Though consumption in the economic sense by no means exhausts this common welfare, the full harmony of economic interests which, as we perceive, cannot emerge through any balance of powers or parties in a Guild or Professional Parliament, can best be found in the organic unity which the physical and spiritual needs and interests of man impose upon economic standards of living. As producer, a man performs one single economic function; as consumer, he brings into personal unity and harmony the ends of all the economic functions. That is why in the new Social Order a consumers' State is entitled to direct the flow of new productive power into the several industrial channels, and to form a final court of appeal for the settlement of such conflicting claims and interests of the several industries or professions as cannot be adjusted by the unprincipled compromise or give and take of a purely functional assembly.

But while the interests of the citizen-consumer, which all industrial processes are intended to sub-serve, must be made paramount, there are sound reasons for bringing together into a National Industrial Council the representatives of capital and labour in the various self-governing industries. For though, as we recognise, no final harmony can be evolved in such a body, and no finality could be accorded to its decisions, there are common interests which can be served by free, full, and regular consultation. Even when the interests, either of several trades, or of employer and employed, conflict, such a Council may furnish a useful organ for conciliation or arbitration, and is certainly required as a first court of reference to consider the reactions which the conduct of any single trade, or group of trades, may have upon other trades or groups. The simplest illustration of this need is the competition of the several industries upon the continuous influx of new labour into the labour market and of new capital into the investment market, and the consequent desira-bility of some agreed standardisation of conditions in the several industries which shall enable each to get its necessary nutriment for purposes of growth. The brief-lived experiment towards such a National Industrial Council in 1919 served to bring out in strong relief the wide recognition of the need of a standardisation of the main conditions of labour, especially for wages, hours, and provision against unemployment. But not less important would be the working out of good and equitable conditions for the supply of capital as between different employment in this country and as between internal and overseas employment. Moreover, to such a National Industrial Council must be referred, in the first instance, the discussion of the forms in which the publication of company and other business accounts, which is essential to any effective treatment of the unity of business life, shall be presented and the safeguards that can be devised in order to secure its accuracy.

The vital importance of publicity for business life is not at all adequately realised. In our discussion of incentives it must take the first place as the indispensable condition of clear thinking and good feeling. How ignorance breeds suspicions which paralyse activity has never been so evident as now. War-passion and its accompanying credulity have helped everywhere to poison human relations, but nowhere more conspicuously than in the business world. No sane human co-operation in trade and industry is possible when essential facts relating to the production and distribution of wealth are hidden or falsified. The conflicts between employer and employed, trade and trade, nation and nation, are everywhere fed by ignorance. " All cards on the table " is the first condition for mutual confidence and co-operation where interests are identical, and for pacific and reasonable adjustment where they conflict. The power of a fully informed public opinion as an influence for the prevention of economic abuses, such as profiteering and sweating on the part of employers, ca' canny on the part of workers, has never been tried. For reliable statistics in such vital matters have never been accessible. Suppose that full disclosure of the true assets and the net profits, accompanied, where necessary, by costings of the several processes upon prescribed forms, were made obligatory for all business firms, would not several exceedingly valuable results follow? First, all the loose imputations of " profiteering " would disappear. If the consumer suspected that he was overcharged for any goods by some ring or combine, the place of this " hold up " and the size of the overcharge would be manifest. If workers made a claim for higher wage-rates than the employers held the trade would bear, the issue would be capable of a clear test. Though in many instances the complexity of the analysis would exceed the intellectual competence or the patience of the majority, there would be skilled and trusted agents and authorities who would expound, and whose accepted exposition would substitute knowledge for mystery. Most educated persons in this country, for example, believe that the critical attack on the present capitalist system by socialists and other " agitators " is. unjust and unreasonable, that is to say, they deny that the capitalist and employing classes are plundering the worker and the consumer. Now so long as the conflict is waged in general phrases about profiteering, sweating, surplus value, and monopoly, no issue is possible. But if these phrases could be submitted to the close test of measured fact, a truly " scientific " analysis of the operations of the industrial system would be obtainable. Skilled accountancy and publication of its results are probably the most immediately urgent of all large reforms. They would not merely have the effect of dissolving or confirming suspicion. Two other results would ensue. The deterrent effect of an informed public opinion upon the abuses of economic power would be itself considerable. Even as matters stand at present a strong trust or combine is accustomed to consider how far it may safely use its power to overcharge consumers, having regard to the ill-will of the public and the possibility of legal intervention. How much stronger would be this restraining power, if the extent of its overcharges and its total gains were public property?

The other result of such accountancy and publicity would be a general levelling up of technique and administration in the several industries, which would at once impel the feebler, less efficient units either to improve or disappear, and would bring the survivors into closer business relations, by reason of their common knowledge of one another and the recognised utilities of combination. It may be said that this higher and closer organisation of the businesses in a trade might bode ill to the consumer. But, as we have seen, the process is going on rapidly at present, but in secret. And, if secrecy can be made to give way to publicity, the necessary protection of consumers against abuses of trade combination can be made far more effective. Organisation represents a higher and more economical condition for a trade than free blind competition, and only under such organisation can any real security for the vital interests of weaker parties, whether workers or consumers, be attained.

But it is needless to labour the question whether some considerable community of interests exists within the area of national industry. So far as this community does exist, the new Industrial Order manifestly requires that it should be represented in some organ, and a National Industrial Council is the proper organ. Nor need it be merely a consultative body, bringing together, as it were, and supplementing the discussions of such bodies as the Congress of Chambers of Commerce and the Congress of Trades Unions. When firmly established it might well be invested with certain regulative and administrative powers for the realisation of the " common good " of industry. But the essential sovereignty of Parliament as the final legislative and executive power in the industrial sphere, as in others, must be maintained. While the required publication of accounts would doubtless need obligatory legislation, by way of amendment of the existing Companies Acts, or otherwise, the deliberations in a National Industrial Council as to the measure, standardisation, instruments and uses of such accountancy would be quite indispensable. For the education which such accountancy would give for the progress of national trade and the expulsion of the common notion that secretiveness is advantageous would be necessary to secure that measure of general consent on the part of business men without which legal provisions would be very difficult to enforce.

We recognise thus that, although a Guild Congress or an Industrial Parliament cannot be entrusted with the supreme government of national industry, some such general organ as a National Industrial Council is an indispensable part of our New Order, though in form and substance it remains subject to the authority of the State.

The ascription of this directing or adjusting function to the State does not, however, imply that from a political organisation there emerges a complete plan or pattern of that economic harmony which the well-adjusted interplay of economic incentives should be designed to secure. The State, as economic adjuster, guarantees no new power or purpose, but acts as an instrument of that economic life which moves and has its being in the system of production and consumption of a community. It is to the evolution of the arts of production and consumption by the wants, desires, and contrivances of men that we look to find the laws of economic life and to discern the creative forces which pulse through its veins. It is in ordered changes of these arts of production and consumption that such economic reconstruction as we are considering consists. But these changes of industrial structure and activity are brought about by changes of incentive. Now these changes of incentive lie mainly in the sphere of distribution, by which we mean the economical apportionment not only of the product but of those streams of effort and enjoyment which are embodied in the concrete goods and services that constitute wealth in the commonly accepted sense. In a well-ordered society this economy of incentives will operate to reduce to a minimum the painful and humanly costly processes of producing wealth and to raise to a maximum the satisfaction attending its consumption.[1] This economy of welfare hinges upon as close a conformity as is possible to the maxim, " From each according to his power, to each according to his needs." All our endeavours to absorb and apply productively the surplus of unearned income, to secure for all workers regular and reliable conditions of employment and subsistence, with access upon easy terms to natural resources and capital, to secure an equitable form of representative government in the essential industries and a social arbitrament for the settlement of conflicting claims of capital and labour, to establish in the State a wise trusteeship over the fresh supplies of capital and labour entering industry—all these efforts are directed to an economy of distribution. The cry, so popular just now among our business men, for more productivity as a separate policy from better distribution, derives from an impatient and short-sighted interpretation of the economic situation. For slack and defective productivity cannot be remedied otherwise than by the stimuli of better distribution. Economy of distribution in its wider sense, the due and economical apportionment, among the several

[1] This doctrine is elaborated in my volume, " Work and Wealth, a Human Valuation " (Macmillan & Co.).

industries and the various productive classes, of the productive energy available for work and of the wealth which is or can be produced, remains the central problem of industrialism.

The failure of our processes of economic reconstruction is due to the breakdown of the incentives which sufficed to keep in tolerable efficiency the co-operative system of productive prices under competitive private enterprise, and to our apparent inability to find an acceptable substitute for the central ordering of our economic life. Hence the many hasty theories and experiments which pass under the name of sovietism, syndicalism, guild-socialism, state socialism, and which, regarded as general schemes of industrial organisation, suffer from the common malady of a weakening of incentives at some centre of activity. The too facile conviction, that private profit can be eliminated from the whole industrial system, that rents and interest can forthwith disappear, that social service can become an inspiring motive for the organisers of industry or the rank and file, that guild harmony of interests among the various grades of brain and hand workers can be easily effected by representative control, and that a functional parliament can legislate satisfactorily for industry as a whole, will disappear before any rigorous analysis of human nature in industry. While nothing can be more certain than that the old arrangements of incentives to efficient industry will no longer work and need to be replaced by new ones, it is equally certain that the psychology of this reform must be adapted to the special technical and human conditions of the several industries, and the types of business in each industry, with close regard to the racial and other natural and educated characters of the employees. Finally, the pace and extent to which reformed industrial methods are capable of application will largely depend upon the education of the general body of citizen-consumers and their willingness to give serious attention to the central processes of industrial government through an intelligently ordered State.